Father Arsenie Boca
Wonderfully Exceptional

Georgeta Germina Punga-Herbreteau

© 2020 Georgeta Germina Punga-Herbreteau/Publisher U2pi

Title: Father Arsenie Boca - *Wonderfully Exceptional*

Author: Georgeta Germina Punga-Herbreteau

Publisher U2pi BV, Den Haag, www.uitgeveriju2pi.nl
Printed by Jouwboekdrukkerij.nl

ISBN: 978-90-8759-941-6
NUR: 700

FATHER ARSENIE BOCA - *WONDERFULLY EXCEPTIONAL*

CONTENTS

FOREWORD

I have issued this present collection of testimonials on the advice and with the blessing of Bishop Daniil Stoenescu of the Diocese of Dacia Felix. It follows my publication of the Dutch translation of the book 'The Path to the Kingdom' by Father Arsenie Boca – an overview of what Father Arsenie had counselled and taught the Romanian faithful through his talks, writings and homilies. The current collection is an attempt to portray this ardent monk who shaped the Orthodox Faith in a unique way and who, to this day, is a guiding source of inspiration to many. Bishop Daniil rightly praises Father Arsenie as 'an Everest Mountain to the Romanian people.'

Dan Lucinescu, renowned author of multiple bestsellers, assured me that every publication on Father Boca, without any doubt, will influence every reader in sublime and mysterious ways. Just as the Christian Faith was a beacon of hope for people during the dark days of the communist occupation of Romania, so too can the teachings and the life of Father Arsenie Boca be a shining example for people today who are weary and crave for a refreshing purification of the soul.

I am grateful to these friends for their encouraging exhortations and practical pieces of advice and I hope that this issue may be an addition to 'The Path to The Kingdom', so that Father

Arsenie can be the man here, as he ever was in Romania: **wonderfully exceptional!**

Finally, I want to thank Neil B. Nucup for his assistance in proofreading and editing my work, Nikodim and my husband Dominique for his patience and trust. Without their valuable cooperation, this work would not have been possible. My unconditional gratitude also goes to Rebeca Bărbulescu, Antonio Gavriluță, Romain Herbreteau and Iulia Nicolau (contributions to the translation), Florin Duțu (photography) and Cezar Buterez (cartography).

Georgeta Germina Punga-Herbreteau
Rijswijk, the Netherlands

Spring 2020

LIKE A LIGHT BULB'S GLOWING FILAMENT

Our all-beloved Father Arsenie Boca (1910-1989) is one of the brightest shining filaments of today's Romanian spiritual 'enlightenment'. Indeed, his charismatic appearance is reflected to this day as 'a pure river of water of life, clear as crystal, proceeding from the throne of God and of the Lamb.' (Revelation 22:1) In his book *Revelation*, or the *Apocalypse*, the apostle John writes, on behalf of Jesus Christ, seven letters to the seven churches in Asia Minor (Revelation 2-3) in which he repeatedly makes in one final verse a divine promise to those who triumphantly end the invisible, spiritual battle.

Father Arsenie has undeniably achieved such a victory through his unwavering faith, his indefatigable commitment and his exemplary life, following the lives of the Egyptian Desert Fathers and the Philokalia.

That is why Father Arsenie is blessed, because 'To him who overcomes I will give to eat from the tree of life, which is in the midst of the Paradise of God.' (Revelation 2:7)

Another reason why Father Arsenie is blessed, is reflected on the verse 'He who overcomes shall not be hurt by the second death.' (Revelation 2:11)

Father Arsenie is blessed a third time because 'To him who overcomes I will give a white stone and on the stone a new name written which no one knows except him who receives it.' (Revelation 2:17)

Father Arsenie is blessed a fourth time because 'He who overcomes, and keeps My deeds until the end, to him I will give authority over the nations; and he shall rule them with a rod of iron, as the vessels of the potter are broken to pieces, as I also have received from My Father; and I will give him the morning star.' (Revelation 2:26-28) Here, the light of the morning star can be interpreted as the Uncreated[1], Divine Light that shines through the soul.

Father Arsenie is blessed a fifth time because 'He who overcomes shall be clothed in white garments, and I will not blot out his name from the Book of Lives, but I shall confess his name to My Father and to His angels.' (Revelation 3:5)

Father Arsenie is blessed a sixth time since 'He who overcomes, I shall make him a pillar in the temple of My God, and he shall no more go out of it and I will write on him the name of My God and the name of the city of My God, the New Jerusalem which comes down out of heaven from My God. And I will write on him My new name.' (Revelation 3:12)

---

1 It is the Light of Tabor in which Christ appeared with Moses and Elijah.
Sometimes believers see it manifested through their human eyes, as "a touch of Divine Eternity on their spirit" (Father Sophrony of Maldon, See God as He Is, Editions du Cerf, 2004).

Indeed, how great is the happiness of those who may dwell eternally in God's House and bear His Name!

Father Arsenie is blessed a seventh time because 'To him who overcomes I will grant to sit with Me on My throne, as I also overcame and sat down with My Father on His throne.' (Revelation 3:21)

†Daniil

Bishop of Dacia Felix

Hăţăgel, 26 September 2018

AUTOBIOGRAPHY

I was born on 29 September 1910 in Vaţa de Sus, a village in the district Hunedoara. I got my first name 'Zian Vălean'[1] from my parents. I went to school in Brad, a town in the same county. By then, I already realized that I enjoyed being on my own. That is why I frequently withdrew into the loneliness of the forests and

---

1 Zian, Transylvanian given name is the abbreviation of Sânzienelor (the feast day on which the birth of Saint John the Baptist is celebrated). According to his biography he was thus baptized, says his biography, because he was the fruit of the prayer of his parents, like Saint John the Baptist.

fields of my village. Religion fascinated me immensely so much so that I asked myself many questions and always went looking for answers. I also had another copy of 'The Religion within the Limits of Pure Reasoning', a book written by the German philosopher Immanuel Kant and published in 1793. I signed it with 'Boca Zian, fourth class Lyceum'.

While I was at secondary school, my father Joseph died. He was a hardworking shoemaker who brought me up really well. I still remember how he disciplined me for wasting time. I then promised him, with tears in my eyes, that it would never happen again. It was an unforgettable and helpful lesson for the rest of my life. At the Avram Iancu Lyceum, I enjoyed math, physics, religion, art and music. That is why, after obtaining my diploma, I thought about specializing in the natural sciences and registering for a course at the Aviation School in Cotroceni. However, this course was too expensive, for which reason I decided to follow my religious calling. In 1929, I enrolled in a course at the Theological Academy in Sibiu.

I was able to afford my theological schooling, thanks to the proceeds from the sale of my parents' house. Moreover, I also had a scholarship. I never asked my mother Christina for help. My parents got divorced in 1922 and my mother lived by herself since then. Under the divorce decree – I was 12 years old at that time – custody over me was granted to my father. He had a fixed income and could pay for my education.

While studying theology, I discovered the beauty of monkhood and through practice I wanted to focus on the mystical side of life. That was why I left my mother and she got used to a life without me. I took as little contact with her as possible. I thought that if I slowly disappeared out of her life, that would at least alleviate the pain the moment I finally withdrew from the world as a monk. During those days, I also imposed upon myself the discipline of austerity. I decided not to meet any more girls. I accomplished this partially, as at the beginning of my theological studies, the ministry also allowed girls to follow the theological course. I never had girlfriends in the city. I consciously abstained from any opportunity to go out. I would only meet up with friends upon the invitation from the Academy and in the presence of a professor. I could not dance nor did I want to learn how to. In fact, I never did. I found it to be inappropriate for a theologian. I also had no interest in what others did outside of class hours, leaving me completely indifferent.

I was mainly concerned with the relationship between the senses, the will and the comparative study of mysticism in world religions. Through study and experience, I wanted to understand how and to what extent willpower can influence the spiritual and biological aspects of life and whether reflexes and instincts could not be controlled by one's consciousness, as the textbooks at that time wrongly stated. During this self-study, I was tremendously helped by the writings and findings of Mircea Eliade who was sent to Calcutta by the University of Bucharest to follow Eastern studies. I saw this study as preparation for the monkhood.

All my activities then, just like today, were purely focused on the inner, never on the outer. That is why I chose and still do, to remain silent over talking. That is why I also carry Arsenie as monk name: I aspire to live spiritually according to the example of Abba Arsenios[2] who had chosen the asceticism of silence, thereby acquiring inner perfection. My efforts resulted in a thesis 'Challenges of the Spiritual Life' (*Încercări asupra vieții duhovnicești*), with which I successfully finished my theological education in Sibiu in 1933.

During the holidays, I dedicated my time to painting, a talent given by God and which was noticed by Metropolitan Nicolae Bălan of Transylvania. He sent me to the Art Academy in Bucharest where I finished the painting course in 1938 without skipping one class. After that, with the blessing of Metropolitan Nicolae, I departed for the Mountain Athos where I stayed for a few months in the Romanian skete Prodromos[3] to further immerse myself into the Orthodox monastic life. (…) Back in Romania I travelled to Chișinău to learn the technique of gilding.

---

2 Holy Abba Arsenios the Great (+ 449, Rome) was a Desert Father in Egypt.
3 The Romanian skete of Prodromos [dedicated to Saint John the Baptist] is a dependance of the Monastery of the Great Lavra of Mount Athos.

Then, I entered the Brâncoveanu Monastery in Sâmbăta de Sus in the county Braşov where I was ordained a monk on the first Friday after Easter in 1939. For two years' time I was the only monk and therefore, I was held responsible for all jobs. For painting there was not enough time. I feared that my talent would be fruitless and that my education in Bucharest was in vain.

Many people came to visit the monastery to find solace and wisdom. Thank God! There came reinforcement. Serafim Popescu became my fellow monk. I asked him to accept the ordination of the priest in my place, for I felt unworthy. The flow of visitors continued and the monastery experienced a spiritual revival. Countrymen came to visit us from far and wide to relay their spiritual problems to us. That was why I, too, was ordained a priest in 1942 and was able to show them the Path to the Kingdom. I could tell them about Jesus Christ, true God and true man, the God-man who showed the way to salvation and sanctification in word and in deed. I was able to teach people to get up after falling into sin and to further complete their path of life with boundless love for others and above all, God Almighty.

That was my only aspiration. That is also my only job.
Monk Arsenie
Râmnicu Vâlcea
17 July 1945

Source: www.fundatiaarsenieboca.ro/biografie

- But not you, right? You are not married? How did you become a deacon?

- I promised during my ordination as deacon that I would live a celibate life. Vader Porphyry, did you bring the pulley that I asked you to bring with you when you went to the wooden mill next to Iviru? If we don't have the pulley, we have to make one using rudimentary tools.

- Rudimentary? I don't know that word! I have never read it in a prayer book or a life of saints.

- Rudimentum, pavimentum, ornamentum, postamentum, testamentum, instrumentum, sacramentum…

- Are you a poet now? No time for jokes! Hold the ax firmly, otherwise we can get hurt badly! Are you ok? Do you think that monastic life on the Athos is easy? Moreover, we suffer from hunger and live in poverty. The help we receive from Romania, is withheld by the Greeks... I believe you, if you say a pulley would limit our efforts. I will steal one tomorrow from Megisti Monastery. There are three pulleys in the workroom!

- Stealing is a sin, Father Porphyry!

Father Dometius had just heard Father Porphyry's last sentence when he returned with a bucket of seawater. Father Porphyry immediately washed his hands and washed his mouth with greedy gulps. I, too, hurriedly refreshed myself, while Father Dometius started the conversation again.

- When you meet the Lord, you rise above yourself and from everything, not only of your injustice but also of your justice. You're living in another, supernatural world, transcendental to all earthly grumbling and chatter. You feel a Celestial serenity unknown to our world.

- Amen, said Porphyry, I didn't know you are so learned. From what 'Fathers Book' did you get those words of wisdom? Like you are not the son of a sheperd from Tilisca, you Dometius.

- From St. Arsenios the Great, the famous hermit in the Scetis desert along the Nile, in Egypt. He rarely spoke, mastered his words and thoughts.

A pleasant silence fell. I suspected Father Porphyry who was less skilled in theology, reflected on the lesson of Father Dometius. They were very meaningful words. Unfortunately, the silence was short-lived.

- My father sent me with the sheep in the mountains. There, in a ravine was a house of a monk from Foltea, Saliste. It was a sort of a rock sheepfold covered with fir decking placed next to each other and covered with soil. Father Achim was short, sort of bandy-legged, with a beard to his knees. He had blue eyes, the color of sea, like you, Zian.

- My mother also had eyes like that. I think I inherited hers. She always hoped that I would become a priest – a married priest – because when I told her that I wanted to become

- Zian Boca, quickly write a letter to your mother. If you forsake that, she will soon die and you will have had her death on your conscience. I know that you are still a virgin and that you avoid dealing with women, but you must be proud because you have a talent for painting and because you were allowed to cut open bodies during your medical studies in Bucharest. Fast, pray, and cut a hundred sticks from a greenhouse tree as a fine to reconcile yourself with God.

We noticed how the rock was almost pulled up or pushed up by itself. Next to us stood 'someone', probably a person, with a beard to the ground and wild hair like the lion's men. We were not really scared, but were surprised, or better yet astonished. Then we heard that soft voice again. "We must praise you truly, O Mother of God." We sang together. My inexperienced voice suddenly had unprecedented melodic bows and vibrations. Father Porphyry sang the base voice in an unheard-of manner and Father Dometius also surpassed himself. The three of us prayed to the Mother of God while a stranger assisted us in an unearthly way. His voice reminded me of the tenor from the cathedral choir of Bucharest. He sang like an angel, not showy, not artificial, but unbelievably cheerful and fluent. It was a truly unique experience. Four individuals sang a hymn to the Mother of God on a rock that stood out over the wild sea. Like the figurehead of a ship, floating above the wild waves. In my mind I saw my mother on her knees crying and praying for the icon of the Mother of God in our cottage in Vața de Sus. She was holding a photo of me in her hands. At that time I was still a child, but I still remember the image very sharply. It is engraved in my memory... The mysterious figure must have read my mind.

- Your mother's name is Creștina. She is now a widow. At your birth she has entrusted you at God and His Church.

I shivered at the thought of standing next to a saint. He was without a doubt a prophet. He knew my name and my past. Father Porphyry was also apparently worried a bit. He asked the question, which burned on everyone's lips, but to which there was no answer...

- Father, what is your name? Who are you? What are you doing here?
- Don't be afraid of Father Abbot Arsenie. He will not punish you because you were absent from Vespers. By the way, do you know that the nine columns of the Athos will come to Easter this year to attend the Holy Liturgy in the small convent of Prodromos? One of them is Father Matthew from Karacalu who celebrates the Liturgy everyday in places where an antimins is available. He will continue to do so until his death. This year it will snow at the top of Mount Athos at Easter. We will therefore see each other again. Brother Zian, don't forget to write to your mother.

Christian Faith. Reading, painting, gardening and praying, that was his life. But he preferred to read…

Father Arsenie was a very good student in high school in Brad. Not only was he interested, but he likewise excelled in every subject. He seemed serious and introvert as though he were too mature for his age. Nevertheless, the spontaneous and childishness occasionally broke through this closed cocoon. I remember that my mother sometimes gave him the task to get eggs in the hen house. He often could not resist the temptation to eat a few in a hurry, which my mother always noticed. "Whoever wants cookies is not allowed to eat the eggs at the hen house!" How many times Zian heard these words! His mischievous eyes always glowed, accompanied by a cheeky smile on his face.

At the Theological Faculty, however, he became even more serious and more introvert. He became more mature, he laughed extremely rarely. It seemed like he was withdrawing himself from the world. During the holidays, he wandered through our village in silence. For hours he could sit in the garden dreaming or thinking under the old pear trees. He also often liked to discuss with my father with whom he had a good relationship. They exchanged enthusiasm with each other, tried to convince each other, but never ending up in disagreement or fight.

As the years went by, Zian became more straightforward, convinced and self-aware in a certain way. He challenged every form of sin and injustice, whoever was guilty. At that point, he was uncompromising and spared no one. He knew that sin could bear the seed of disaster in it. However, he remained very kind and tender to his family, but he was still strict. I remember how my father Vasile, we called him 'Lică,' one evening suggested Zian to drink a glass of brandy, which of course Father Arsenie immediately refused. Hence, he comforted my father immediately, "Lică, please enjoy e glass of brandy, without me!"

As I earlier mentioned, Father Arsenie was very introvert and withdrawn during his youth. He hardly looked and made any contact. My parents had a lot of godchildren in the church. It gave them a lot of joy when they were invited to their wedding or later to the baptism of their children. My mother always asked Zian to accompany her to the party: "Zian, come with us to the party. You are young, you can dance there and have fun…" Every time, Zian gave her the same answer: "Ah, Mărioară, Mărioară, don't you worry. I was not made for this world!" That was also true. Father Arsenie was different. He wanted to be alone, he only wanted to serve Christ. He did not want his overly friendly dealings with people to interfere with his personal relationship with Christ and interfere with his task. That is why he chose to avoid not only girls and women, but also boys and gentlemen.

When his homily was over, he walked through the mass of people. He looked at them and briefly told them what they needed and what they had to do. Then he came to my direction. His gaze fathomed me and his voice spoke to me: "Child, fulfil your military service and then visit me again. We will then talk about monastic life." I was nailed to the ground. I did not know what to say. The thought of becoming a monk had never occurred to me, but after seeing and hearing it, it did not even seem like a bad idea, especially with him and in his monastery!

He was not muscular, but tall and quite skinny. He seemed fragile and strong at the same time. His gaze was energetic, his attitude was convincing. Father Boca radiated determination in a calm and pleasant manner. He did not have to overwhelm anyone with many words or emphatic gestures. His voice and eyes spoke calmly, but still commanding respect on what had to be done or left alone. He was strict and inexorable. He wanted to get rid of sin and lead people to the path to a better life and virtuous behaviour. Those who followed his advice only noticed how beneficial his advice actually was.

To his young monks, Father Boca was an inspiring abbot. He loved teaching us all kinds of different things – from literature and iconography to bricklaying and working in the stable. He worked with us laughing. He often told jokes and he never demanded impossible things. He knew the limits of every monk even though there was a lot of work that had to be done. The monastery was a ruin. For years it had been destroyed due to being unused before he started the reconstruction. Many students came to help unasked. He often and happily played with them in the snow. "It's good to play now, later your life will become serious enough. Then you will have no more time."

It is difficult to explain what Father Arsenie was like during the Holy Liturgy. He was like a magnet that brought us all around him and led us to Christ. We felt surrounded by a force that was not of this world and through which we forgot all our earthly worries. Truly, I have travelled a lot. I have met many people, but no one was as intense as Father Arsenie Boca. As a person and as a priest, he only regarded himself as an instrument through which the Holy Spirit worked. "Do not look at me like that!" It was a warning that many people were allowed to hear. Undoubtedly, it was also this solidarity in the Holy Spirit that reunited the believers again and again during the memorial services to Father Arsenie...

Family was extremely important to Father Boca. "Why do we call God Our Father? Why is it a divine command to honor our parents by being obedient to them?" Every father and mother wishes their son or daughter to live a dignified and virtuous life. Righteousness and respect for God's creation, for each person and every animal and everything, are indispensable for a better future. Is it not the task of humanity to sustain the world? That at home when my sister 'invited' me, in a quite compelling way, to accompany her to Brâncoveanu Monastery, near Făgăraş (Transylvania). Admittedly, I was not so enthusiastic about her invitation. In fact, I was mad and in distress because I could not concentrate on my studies as much I wanted to.

Hundreds of young adults, girls and boys were sitting in the orchard of the monastery around the exceptionally handsome monk. He was dressed in a white, lamb's wool outfit with a wide, black, leather belt. The belt buckle had a large X. His shiny black hair and relatively small beard made his face attractive, but the piercing stare of his bright blue eyes was unmistakably unique. In all honesty, I was not in the mood to listen intently to this man and even thought that he was an impostor who only wanted to make the girls' hearts run wild. That was why I left the group and leaned against a young tree in order to watch the scene from a safe distance. How was it possible that a group of university students, who belonged to the Romanian elite, listened to a monk who told them stories? He talked about *The Flame*, a novel by the Swedish writer Selma Lagerlöf. I read the book a long time ago. It was the story of a young prince, the son of the Doge of Venice, who grew up in extreme luxury. He was spoiled and admired by the richest women, and went constantly from party to party. One night, he promised in a drunken mood that he would bring a flaming torch from the Holy Grail in Jerusalem. He kept his promise and departed in beautiful clothes on a beautiful rigged horse to the Holy Land.

After years of wandering and adventure, he returned on a donkey and as a totally destitute beggar. Nobody seemed to recognize him. Only the burning flame reminded the Venetians of the earlier promise that was fulfilled. The young man spent his further life as a Christian in simplicity and humility. After his death, he was declared a saint.

I noticed how the students listened to his story, filled with emotions and intense attention. After the story, Father Arsenie said that he would take a little break before continuing the conversation and also providing a chance to answer questions. He stood up and left the round hill on which he and his audience were sitting. To my great surprise, I saw him walking to my direction. He stopped next to me and put his hand on my shoulder. He looked at me and asked: *"Tell me, Dan. Honestly. Do you really think I am an impostor?"*

I was in shock. How did he know who I was and what I thought? I was here in the monastery for the first time. Nobody knew me. My shy, introvert sister was nowhere to be found, and next to me stood an amiable monk reading my thoughts and correcting me. I looked at Father Arsenie, embarrassed and asked for forgiveness and prayed in silence to get me out of that uncomfortable situation. He smiled, kept his hand on my shoulder and asked if I wanted to stay longer in the monastery, as he would like to continue talking to me. I nodded and we walked through the orchard to the monastery. I have to add out of the train carriage, the coachman arrived at the platform and invited her to step into the carriage that would take her to the monastery. Upon her arrival, she recognized the beauty of the landscape and the buildings. She had already seen these images in her dreams when she carried her unborn child in her lap.

Father Arsenie ate very little to everyone's surprise although he did a lot of work. He also 'celebrated' every fast as a party. His traditional food for fasting consisted of raw, sometimes grated, carrots. His reverence for the Liturgy, the Gospel, and the Bloodless[2] Sacrifice was exceptionally high. He liked talking and often about the mysterious and mystical nature of the Liturgy. Reading the Gospel out loud was an immense privilege, and praying and experiencing the Epiclesis (Consecration)[3] brought Father Arsenie in tears. He wept because he began to experience the transcendent greatness of God at that unique moment.

That was exactly why he could not stand sin, but with the greatest possible love he embraced all people who pursued purity and humility. He also helped everyone who wanted to spread the Christian faith in word and deed. For example, in 1942, he visited Castle Bran where Princess Ileana, the sister of King Carol II, built a hospital. He was asked to dedicate the

---

2 I.e. the Eucharist!
3 During the Epiclesis, according to the Orthodox rite, it is the Holy Spirit Himself who descends on the Gifts to sanctify them.

Orthodox chapel in it, in the courtyard of the castle. When the Russian troops occupied the country and King Michael was forced to give up the throne, she refuged to the United States. There she founded an Orthodox monastery, of which she became an abbess, as Mother Alexandra[4].

Father Arsenie often emphasized, through his testimonies, that Jesus comes to earth, unnoticed to share the fate of humanity. Such a case took place in the streets of Bessarabia in 1940. Father Arsenie then learned the technique of finishing the background of an icon with gold leaf or silver. Russia had ordered Romania to leave Bessarabia within two days, although without any discussion, as it was Romanian territory. Although the Romanians immediately took the necessary measurements to flee, after only a day, the Russian tanks crashed into the streets of Bessarabia to block the roads and stop the flow of refugees. Romanian soldiers and officers were shot without any warning. The people started to panic and fled into the fields and forests. They left their horses and carriages behind and could only take the essentials. Father Arsenie also had to flee. He managed to take the last train at Chişinău station and left. Fear and despair made all faces cramp. People had to leave, lest death awaited them in Siberia. Father Arsenie prayed as

---

[4] Mother Alexandra, born Princess Ileana of Romania (1909-1991), great-granddaughter of Queen Victoria of England, daughter of King Ferdinand, became a nun at the Russian convent of Bussy-en-Othe in Burgundy (1961), before going to the USA where she founded the Lord's Transfiguration Monastery in Elwood City, Pennsylvania. Jean-Paul Besse dedicated a beautiful book to her: Jean-Paul BESSE, Ileana de Roumanie, l'Archiduchesse voilée, éditions Via Romana (2010).

hour turned out not to have arrived yet. He entrusted his life and death to God.

The horror took over the country. The number of arrests increased and so did the tension. The poor farming population prayed fearfully for the icons of the Romanian saints, the Mother of God and Christ. Many feared for the apocalypse. Father Arsenie was forced to leave the monastery in Sâmbăta and to go to the monastery of Prislop, an isolated place in the Romanian mountain. While the monastery in Sâmbăta was slowly dying, the monastery was rising in Prislop. Nothing or nobody can stand in the way of the plans of Divine Providence. Inspired by God's grace, Father Arsenie transformed the desolate place into the most visited pilgrimage site in Romania. Prislop was stormed by countless believers who wanted to visit their spiritual father. In Prislop, in the deepest darkness of the night, a flame flared up to illuminate the entire country.

The Security, however, was not disturbed and sought revenge. In January 1951, Father Arsenie was again arrested and an investigation was opened against him. When a cop violently slapped Father Arsenie on the cheek, he got up out of his chair, looked at the man calmly and said earnestly: *"The hand that struck me, will not hit anyone else."*

The aggressive officer made a loud cry, but his hand remained motionless in the air. Father Arsenie was sentenced to fourteen months of forced labor at the construction site of Poarta Albă, a village alongside the channel between the Danube and the Black Sea. This place of damnation grew into a true extermination camp where around 12,000 people died of inhumane treatment, inadequate rest and malnutrition. Father Arsenie was assigned to a group of people who already reached the age of 60. They, too, had to dig out many cubic meters of soil everyday with their hands, with pickaxes or shovels. Many of them were on the verge of mental and physical collapse. The arrival of Father Arsenie brought some relief. He assisted the people who had lost all strength in their arms due to fatigue, and helped them dig. He comforted the sick and desperate, and spoke to them about their loved ones. He also contacted his mother in a hidden, spiritual way in Vața de Sus where the latter lived. The guards treated Father Arsenie with respect and occasionally gave him some peace.

One day, Father Arsenie asked a guard for a few hours of rest and promised to finish his planned work. Because he deeply trusted Father Arsenie, the guard agreed. Shortly thereafter, the order came from above to check the number of detainees. During the counting, it appeared that one prisoner, a monk, was missing. In Poarta Albă, the alarm was sounded, all entrance gates were closed and the counting started again. To everyone's surprise, Father Arsenie now appeared to be present. The responsible officer did not understand. Annoyed, he asked Father Arsenie where he was during the count. Nothing indicated that he had left the camp. His answer surprised everyone: *"During the break for which I received permission, I was at my mother's funeral, near Vața de Sus."*

It was impossible to travel across the Apuseni Mountains in less than two hours to a village, 800 km further away from the prison camp to attend a funeral service, and returned even without leaving any trace behind! When a colonel ordered a thorough investigation on this matter, the spokesperson of the State Security Ministry quickly responded positively. Father Arsenie did attend his mother's funeral!

The next day, the highest commander of the Security ordered Father Arsenie to be released. It was unanimously decided that it would be more sensible to grant Father Arsenie his freedom and to keep an eye on him, than to lock him up in a cell where he nevertheless can escape on his own initiative to go and come in when it suited him.

Halfway through 1952, Father Arsenie arrived again in the monastery of Prislop. However, he realized that the joy would be short-lived. The monastery would not escape the heavy oppression. A short time later, the monastery was indeed claimed: it became a retirement home for the elderly and the nuns were asked to leave the monastery. They were allowed to only take their personal belongings. The personal secretary of the Bishop of Arad handed Father Arsenie a letter with the episcopal logo. This official deed prohibited Father Arsenie from further wearing spiritual clothing in the future and from exercising the functions of a priest. He may choose, as a free citizen, wherever he wanted to go, but the secretary advised him to get in his car to leave the monastery immediately and avoid further contact with the Security.

Father Arsenie suddenly became a homeless wanderer without any means of subsistence. The country suffered during the occupation. Everyone, rich and poor, young and old, educated and illiterate, felt how the unbearable burden of evil weighs on everyday life. People tried to help each other. Father Arsenie was also offered a job. He was hired as a painter at the Romanian Patriarchate in Bucharest. There were many stories about this period of Father Arsenie's life and they were told by the believers who visited him. For example, a Theology student who later wanted to become and did become a priest, asked Father Arsenie to paint an icon for him. Later, when Father Arsenie gave him this icon, he warned the future priest: *"Take care of this icon because he has a special grace."* Later, the student witnessed as he was driving on his scooter through a rain shower with this icon, everything was wet, but his icon remained dry for some reason.

Father retired in 1968. He went to Drăgănescu, a village near Bucharest and started the restoration of the Nicholas Church. A monumental task awaited him. The entire interior would be taken care of and Father Arsenie would be responsible for both the design and the execution of the restoration. After the monasteries of Sâmbăta and Prislop, this would be the third meeting point where believers can speak to Father Arsenie and worship the icons of so many saints from ancient and new times. The village church in Drăgănescu was for the Romanian Orthodox believer as the Sistine Chapel was for the Roman Catholic believer: an anchorage of peace in a hectic world.

Father Arsenie was a visionary, without any doubt. He saw the future, both of people and of regions or countries. Is it not surprising, therefore, that an inside wall of the church gives a glimpse of the contemporary world with objects that did not yet exist in those days? A space shuttle, a wireless phone, satellites. One can even distinguish two towers that merge into a cloud of dust at a relatively small distance from each other. It is impossible to look at this scene without thinking of the destruction of the Twin Towers in New York on 11 September 2001. What appeals most, however, is the portrayal of the risen Christ: full of Love and radiating a Heavenly Light. He looks at the viewer invitingly: "And you, who do you say I am?" God and man, the God-man, God with us.

Shortly before finishing this great work at the Nicholas Church in Drăgănescu, Father Arsenie built his own atelier and cell in the monastic establishment in Sinaia where he spent his final days on earth. He lived as a saint and died as a saint. There were many opinions about his death on 28 November 1989. I suspect he was killed by two members of the security police. Did he foresee his own death when he depicted a crucified monk on a wall in the church of Drăgănescu? Maria Dumitraşcu testified that a woman, probably Elena Ceauşescu[5], planned the death of Father Arsenie. Father Horia, who lived close to Father Arsenie, had knowledge about a meeting with high personalities, to which meeting Father Arsenie was 'invited'. He was brutally pushed into the car and taken to an unknown place where he was probably abused. His hands were maimed, only his right index finger was intact. His cheeks showed circular burn marks of about 2 cm and his face had green-yellow traces of blows. Father Arsenie died in the monastic establishment of Sinaia. Father Bunescu, a priest, washed Father Arsenie and put on his priestly robes, which he had not worn since 1959. He was taken immediately to the Prislop Monastery where he was buried on 4 December 1989. There he rests in a simple grave in a place that he himself has chosen.

---

5 The wife of Nicolae Ceauşescu, communist dictator of Romania.

Epilogue

Every story about Father Arsenie is incomplete. Nobody can fully tell the life story of a person, certainly not the story of such a wonderful man as Father Arsenie. We can only pray to him that he would pray for us to God. He was a saint with remarkable gifts. He was able to read the present, the past and the future of every person. He knew their sins and their talents, and healed their souls. He was a unique confessor. He was able to move through time and space unseen as he showed at his mother's funeral. He shared his physical and mental energy with the weak and the suffering in an unprecedented way. He was a visionary priest-monk with a great charisma who could control the evil and opposing forces. He fought against sin because as he testified, it can work through for three generations. *(A Dutch bundling of his texts appeared in 2018 under the title "The Path To The Kingdom", ed.)*

"We do not come from the monkeys, but we may become them."

"Smoking is unnatural; otherwise, God would have provided a chimney.

"The love of God for the greatest sinner is greater than the love of the greatest saint for God."

"The Holy Liturgy sustains the world."

"The spiritual helm determines the course that we sail, and the final port where we will set foot."

"There are many ways to enter the Kingdom of God, but there is only one door: Jesus."

"God does not ask for miracles, God makes them!"

"Christianity is not just a Sunday affair, but it is a daily effort."

"The truth is not a concept, but a person."

"The longest route runs from the head to the heart."

This text is a compilation of excerpts from the book 'Părintele Arsenie Boca, un sfânt al zilelor noastre' (Father Arsenie Boca, a saint of our time), Publisher Siaj, 2009.

Father STEFAN NEGREANU
Priest-Professor

Stefan Negreanu was born on 24 February 1973. At present, he teaches Orthodox Theology at the Faculty Ilarion V. Felea in Arad.

The centenary of the birth of Father Arsenie was celebrated under the slogan 'A man, exalted above men.' This slogan was not made up, but actually came from the mouth of someone who personally knew Father Arsenie. My brother told me the story that he, himself, heard when he visited the church in Drăgănescu in 1993-1994, accompanied by the 'driver' of Father Arsenie.

When Father Arsenie stayed in the monastery in Prislop, the nuns did not have a car, but they could call upon the services of a driver from a neighboring village. He often brought Father Arsenie to Hațeg, to Hunedoara, or elsewhere where necessary. He told my brother what he, personally, had experienced.

"I have never told anyone this, but maybe it is good that people do know. Sometime in November, I drove back to the monastery with Father Arsenie. It was late autumn, the last leaves fell from the trees. The landscape turned red-brown, the forests rested on the slopes. We arrived at the foot of a slope when the horses suddenly stopped. They were restless, nodding nervously. I did not understand what was happening, nor did I see any obstacle on the road. I took my whip and hit the horses to get them moving again. Father Arsenie ordered me to stop beating the animals in a compelling tone. He stood up and shouted with a loud voice: 'Get out of there!' His voice broke through the silence of the landscape. I did not see anyone and urged my horses to start moving again with my whip. 'Stop hitting!' Father Arsenie looked at me imperatively. Then he turned his eyes to a grove of bushes. 'Get out of there!' I saw a wolf, the size of a calf, running away up the hill.

The horses reacted startled and paralyzed. They no longer moved from their place. Father Arsenie stepped out of my cart, gave the horses a slap on their flank, and stepped up the hill. He stretched out his hands, whistling in a strange way. What happened then cannot be described in words. From the bare forests, hundreds of birds flew in, landing on and around Father Arsenie. What an incredible scene! I really don't know if Father Arsenie carried the birds to the hilltop or the birds brought him there. At the highest point of the slope, he whistled again and the birds retreated to the leafless trees. Then, Father Arsenie turned around laughing and signalling at us: 'Come on!' And the horses started to walk at his words. They pulled my carriage up the hill without any fear."

With tears in his eyes, the driver movingly closed his story: 'This was Father Arsenie. A human being, exalted above the people.'

Another testimony comes from the wife of a warden who guarded Father Arsenie when he had to spend a few months in prison in Braşov. One day, this woman was in the same train compartment as my father-in-law, Father Petru Vamvulescu, when she told him the following story.

"My husband was a guard in Braşov and had to keep an eye on some prisoners. He could watch, day and night, through a peephole in the cell door to see who was in the cell and what was happening. One day, he looked through the hatch of Father Arsenie's cell door. He saw the monk praying on his knees while high flames flared up around him. Although my husband worked at the Securitate, from childhood, he deeply respected the priest and the Church. He unlocked the door, hurried into the cell and, just like the prison guard of Paulus at Philippi (Acts 16, 19-40), fell on his knees with the words: 'I do not know who or what you are, but I do know that you do not belong here. I will make sure that you can leave this place as a free man.' Father Arsenie looked at my husband with his penetrating gaze and replied: 'Friend, I am here, because God wants me to be here. If that had not been the case, I would not have been here now. My place is here. So, go back to your desk, close the door and concentrate on your work.' My husband has told this truly incredible story several times and each time he gets upset and moved, as it seems so surreal."

Another story tells how a prosecutor asked Father Arsenie which prayer is most effective, which prayer God prefers to hear. Father Arsenie answered him: "Every prayer is good, but prayers in which a person puts his whole soul please God the most. I was at the altar of the church in Drăgănescu when a woman entered the church. She looked around to make sure there were no people present. She had not seen me. I remained quiet and saw her kneel in the middle of the church to touch the ground with her face while she cried out: 'God, save me! God save me! God, don't leave me!' That was a true prayer – without any nice words, but real and genuine. Someone can delightfully sing Psalms or Akathists and impress the audience, yet they cannot reach God. What is important is the heart, the inspiration with which people pray…"

This is an excerpt from the book "Părintele Arsenie Boca, un om mai presus de oameni" (Father Arsenie Boca, a man exalted above men), Volume 4, Agaton, 2011.

ASPAZIA OȚEL PETRESCU
Political Prisoner

Aspazia Oțel Petrescu was born on 9 December 1923 in Cotul Ostriței, a village in present-day Ukraine. After high school, she attended classes at the Faculty of Literature and Philosophy at the University of Cluj from 1944 to 1948. Her philosophy professor Lucian Blaga described her as a literary talent and encouraged her to keep writing. She also gives a few lectures about 'Jesus in Romanian poetry'. On 9 July 1948, just before her final exam, the Security arrested Aspazia and sentenced her to ten years in prison. Shortly before her release, her prison sentence was extended for another four years. She spent this time in various prisons, namely Miercurea Ciuc, Mislea, Dumbrăveni, Jilava, Botoșani, and Arad. Together with fellow prisoners, she testified about these years: "We have met Christ alive, in moments of true hunger, cold, thirst, loneliness and pain."

After her release in 1962, Aspazia lived in Roman, the city where she, with great effort, managed to build a new life as a typist. After the Romanian revolution in 1989, Aspazia participated in almost all commemorations of martyrs from communist prisons. Together with some other prominent women, she managed to build in Mislea a chapel, which was inaugurated on 12 November 1994. It was the most important place for the politically condemned girls and women who experienced cold and hardship in communist prisons. Aspazia died on 23 January 2018.

Whoever experiences God's presence can only cry tears of joy and gratitude for the palpable and overflowing love that surrounds and permeates everything and everyone. Words to describe this experience are unnecessary as they are always insufficient.

I got to know Father Arsenie through my friend Zorica Laṭcu. She wrote Christian poetry and was tutored by Nichifor Crainic. Later, she entered the monastery as nun Theodosia. She suggested going together to the monastery at Sâmbăta de Sus. I needed a confessor and she knew Father Arsenie. We were on our way, the two of us, by foot, through snow that reached up to our bellies. It was a winter night in February 1948. It was a long way from Sâmbăta de Jos to Sâmbăta de Sus, but giving up was a word that Zorica did not know. Although she was handicapped, she kept a constant pace. I, on the other hand, could hardly keep up with her. I suspected that the love for Father Arsenie and his monastery gave her strength. The road was hidden under the meter-high snow carpet, a winding road had been created that led us to the monastery, maybe by the monks or maybe by previous visitors. When we arrived, there was no one to be seen. Zorica hurried to the monks and to her room. (She had her own cell in the monastery, probably because she often visited). I was warmly welcomed by a nun and was able to withdraw for a while to wash and braid my hair. She advised me not to leave my head uncovered as soon as I came to the monks. I thanked her for her advice and began to cry uncontrollably.

- Why are you crying? Have you seen Father Arsenie?
- No, sister. I don't know him, I don't even know what he looks like.
- Then he has seen you!
- How can the father see me? I do not understand you…
- Zorica must have talked to Father Arsenie about you!

To me, it all felt very strange, but also impressive. Then, a monk came to us. He asked me to accompany him to Zorica's room. The wood stove was just lit. An open window tried to expel the smoke from the room.

- You can close the window as soon as the smoke has disappeared. Soon it will become warmer. Zorica asked you to wait for her here. Yes?
- Of course, father. Of course, I will wait for her.

He quietly left the room. With my coat loose over my shoulders, I stood in front of the open window and admired the winter landscape. Everything was spotless white. Nothing seemed to be touched by humans. The huge mountains suddenly looked so fragile. An old, arid stump in the garden now served as an incense burner. A thin line of smoke circled almost straight up through the thin air. It was a quiet white morning, a landscape for angels. Holiness, heaven nearby, I cried.

- Why are you crying? What is going on?

It scared me, although it was a warm, soft voice with an accent from Transylvania, which unexpectedly pulled me away from my daydream. For a moment, I lost my balance out of bewilderment, but the hand of an attentive monk held me up.

- Why are you scared? You wanted to meet me right?

I tried to find my peace again. It must be Father Arsenie. I expected a rough, short voice. People called him 'the scourge of God' because he disciplined sinners. He was merciless according to the book. I turned around and saw a tall figure standing in front of the doorway. When he came closer, I noticed his extremely beautiful face. It did not show an earthly beauty, but rather a shine of serenity and holiness, which was emphasized by his bright blue eyes, a gaze with an almost endless depth.

- Why are you so scared? I am determined to free you from your fear. I want to help you get out of the darkness and lead you to the Path of the Lord. Welcome!

Doubt overwhelmed me. I thought, 'My God, what have I done now? Why did I come here? Whom did I want to meet? Where do I find the power to confess my sins honestly and openly?' The monk read my thoughts, expressed my hesitation and gave me courage.

- Hold on, do not run away and do not apologize. Do not be afraid. Once freed from the chains of the Evil One, you still have a long way to go with obstacles. The more energetically you follow this path, the harder the obstacles are that the adversary throws at you.
Do not give up! Never! Now go eat something, and then we will continue talking...

Just a few moments later, Zorica showed up while Father Arsenie disappeared unseen. I sat on the bed to recover and catch up. I loved being here, but it was also very surprising. The ambiguous feeling did not fade away during lunch. I saw Zorica discussing with Father Arsenie. Together they were working on a Philokalia project. I looked around and did not notice how Father Arsenie came to me and put his hand on my wrist.

- You have to be brave here. Now, you need to catch your breath here, spiritually. Soon, during the Holy Week, you will be back. Then we will talk and you can confess fearlessly.

Then, we tear up the diabolical letter of debt and you will be freed from the burden of sin, which the devil stacks on your back. Then you will have the power to tell everything and free yourself completely.

It was early February and the Feast of the Presentation of our Lord God[1] was over. I felt liberation, but also shame. I felt the need for a confessor, but I never asked for a holy priest. How can I entrust my sins to him? I felt suffocated, not because of the snow, but because of the intense warmth that it exuded. I was scared and remained scared.

At the end of April, I returned to the monastery in Sâmbăta de Sus, with Zorica. It was spring and Palm Sunday. Many visitors wanted to attend the Liturgy. Some would stay there to experience the services of the Great and Holy Week with the monks. The future Metropolis was already there and so was the student who would later be very meaningful for Father Arsenie as 'Mother Zamfira.' Father Arsenie led the Liturgy. He sang lively and penetratingly, not spectacularly, but with a voice that carried the songs and made them resonate, especially in this mountain landscape full of spring air where nature sang along, celebrated and prayed along.

In the church, Father Arsenie stood by the altar in Christ's presence and power. That was undeniably tangible. Father

1 Also called Hypapante or Candlemas, Feast of the Presentation of Jesus in the Temple.

Arsenie cried while saying the words of the Epiclesis[2]. I couldn't hear it in his voice, but I saw his shoulders shake gently. It was touching, movingly beautiful. The churchgoers also cried, all of them, whether they came there more often or they were there for the first time. When and where the Holy Spirit comes, every word was redundant and every resistance was broken. Then there were only the tears – tears of relief, of liberation, of gratitude, of emotion. I sang with a broken voice, while the tears were rolling down my cheeks.

Father Arsenie assigned me Zorica's cell to stay there on Monday, Tuesday and Wednesday. The other visitors, including my neighbor and good friend Maria Leşanu from Cernăuţi, were accommodated in the common room. I received a prayer book and also his bundled texts, 'The Path To The Kingdom.' He asked me to read from a literary point of view the chapter about King David and the sin he committed and about which he repented to a great extent. I prayed and read. Then came the message that I was allowed to confess on Thursday.

I must confess that I felt immense shame and great fear of Father Arsenie. However, that seemed premature. My heart opened and my mouth told everything without hesitation, without impediment. Father Arsenie asked me to speak to my father, to tell him to come here, but I never

---

2 Invocation of the Holy Spirit on Holy Gifts. In the Orthodox Church, it is through the epiclesis that the consecration of the Holy Gifts is accomplished.

transmittted this invitation to my father. I also trusted Father Arsenie that I was thinking of entering the monastery.

- That's nice. How sure are you?
- It is my wish, Father, but I still have some doubts.
- A little?
- A little bit. 1%...
- And why?
- Because I am not sure that this is really my calling. Maybe God has another plan for me and I don't want to make the mistake of renouncing my final assignment.

Father Arsenie smiled. For the first time I saw him laughing sweetly, carefree and spontaneously. It was a disarming moment. His answer was disarming and broke every resistance, every doubt.

- Do not forget, girl, that this one per cent is just as important as everything else together... What are we going to do? We are going to present this question of life to the Mother of God. Let us pray together to receive a clear answer to this question. I pray here in the monastery and you in your home. Come back to the monastery at the Feast of the Dormition of the Mother of God[3]. Then we will have an answer that is beyond any uncertainty. What she states and does is God's Will. I assure you.

3 Commemoration (August 15) of the peaceful death of the Mother of God and her ascent to Heaven.

I was relieved and very satisfied. The entire burden seemed to have fallen off or taken away from my shoulders. The confession lasted long, very long. Father Arsenie did not give me an epitemy[4]. He forgave me all my sins so that I could immediately receive communion. Nevertheless, I consciously avoided Father Arsenie the following days - maybe, for fear that my many reprehensible sins left a dark trail in his memory.

That Thursday evening, after the service of the Twelve Gospels,[5] Father Arsenie invited Zorica and me for an extensive meal. After all, people no longer ate on Good Friday and Silent Saturday. They were two days of strict fasting. As we left the church, Father Arsenie led the way. He carried a short, thick candle in his hands to enlighten the path to the refectory. There was a heavy storm, as it often happened between the mountains. Heavy snowflakes were blown away by the strong wind. We walked through a flapping white curtain. I looked at the candle flame, which seemed to dance, but did not go out. How was that even possible? I almost sprained my foot. My attention did not go to the narrow road, but to the flame. Arriving at the dining room, Father Arsenie handed me the candle when he opened the door. People went up the small stairs. Three, four

---

4 After the confession, the priest (especially the spiritual Fathers in the monasteries) sometimes gives an epitemy (sometimes called a canon) to the faithful, that is to say a task to be accomplished, reading, prayer, action. It is not a punishment, but an act to restore those who confess spiritually and physically in the Church. Father Cleopa Ilie, when he was giving an epitemy to someone, who had just confessed, asked him if he was able to accomplish it. If the latter said that he could not, he gave him a lighter epitemy. (Cf. Ioanichie Bălan, Father Cleopa, The Age of Man, 2004, Page 103)

5 Office of Holy Thursday where we read in the Church twelve extracts from the Gospels of the Passion of Christ.

steps perhaps, I forgot the right number. I tried to protect the candle flame by hand, but to no avail. When I finally entered the dining room as the last one, together with Father Arsenie, I gave him back the candle without a word. He reacted quickly.

- You should be less surprised, ask fewer questions. Learn how to hold the light, it's not easy.

I got scared and did not go into the dining room, but immediately ran to the kitchen. Father Arsenie came after me.

- Where are you going? Did I ask you to come here? Go straight to the dining room.
- Forgive me, Father. I didn't dare stay.
- Go where I told you to go. Sit down with Zorica.

His voice was short and imperative, unexpectedly loud. I sat down at the table, and took a seat next to Zorica. Then Father Arsenie started the table prayer. He was different. He changed. How can I put that into words? Maybe I used a photo as a metaphor, an image as a symbol. Even now, in my old age, I often had the impression that, even in his books, his words not only could be 'heard', but could be 'visualized' as well. What he said and how he said it was a concrete and suggestive experience that is carried with you in your heart and in your memory and that you can recall as a memory. It was just like when one looks at a photo and immediately smells the scent, sees the colours, feels the atmosphere, and hears the sounds that belong to that specific moment.

Father Arsenie talked to Zorica during the meal. For a moment, he turned to me.

- Anyone who disobeys in a monastery will be punished. Therefore, also you. That is why I forbid you to celebrate the resurrection at the cave. You stay in your room to learn and experience what obedience means.

I knew that Father Arsenie had a personal monastery cell near the cave. However, again, I cannot accept his decision because I did not want to miss this service. I secretly made plans to avoid his punishment for me. Maybe, I can let the people leave and join the group a little bit later, unseen next to the church and through the forest, by myself. 'Father Arsenie would never notice me', I told myself.

It was easier said than done. I secretly and unobtrusively walked to the church when I came face to face with Father Justin. Father Arsenie had assigned Father Justin as his substitute. What Father Justin told me was something, with the words that Father Arsenie would use. That was why I had to trust and fully comply with him.

- Sister Aspazia! Did you not have to stay in your room? Has the evil one tempted you to go look secretly for Father Arsenie?

- Yes, Father.

- Father Arsenie has foreseen that and told me so. Because of your second disobedience, I, too, am punished. I must also stay here with you. I have to see that you carry out your punishment. Let's sit here on the bench and talk. Then time passes faster.

A little later Father Arsenie returned. In his footsteps, the monks and the visitors walked with a candle in their hands. The group was enlightened and split the darkness, light and shadow, good and evil. I sat in the dark until they passed by. Father Arsenie looked at me for a long time. I still remember his gaze and his words.

- I will now give you a word that should give direction to your life and continue to give it: those who want to avoid the cross will encounter it in more and more serious situations. You now also try, like the unbelieving Thomas, to approach everything rationally from the doubt, to plan. Of course, you have to think and consult, but that, too, has its boundaries.

The next day, I went to him in the morning. I knelt in front of him. He put his hand on my head and blessed me several times.

- May God bless you, my child. May God bless you. May God bless you. May God bless you.

Stop by the church and take a holy bread (prosphore)[6] for your mother.

I was impressed by the peace and warmth that came from his voice. Also Leonida, who accompanied me, was excited by what she saw.

- I'm so surprised and happy. Have you seen how many times Father Arsenie has blessed you? Did you count that?
- No, absolutely not.
- I think he has blessed you for every problem that will force itself on you...

It was true. I really thought Father Arsenie saved me from a great deal of disaster at that moment. He did not take it all away, but made it more bearable and bent it to my advantage. I was in prison and one evening I heard a familiar voice in a dream image. A man was beaten above me. He screamed out of pain and begged not to be tortured any further. I thought it was my father's voice. I knelt down and prayed:

---

6 Liturgical rolls, made from flour, water and sourdough used in the Orthodox Church for the Eucharist. From these prosphora the priest takes morsels for the living and the dead who are commemorated during the Liturgy, and who are thus associated with the Communion in the Chalice.

- Lord, let me serve my father's sentence. He is old and can no longer tolerate the pain. Let his sorrow become my sorrow.
Save him this effort.

However, I later reflected on my decision. Have I not acted against God's will? Why did I ask something like that? I doubted, did not know what to do with myself. Then Father Arsenie appeared to me in a dream. He was dressed in a radiant, white robe.

- What are you worried about, my child? You have acted well. And what you have asked then, is still waiting for you. Know that God takes every gesture of forgiveness very seriously. How much greater than not His joy, if you also take someone's punishment! Certainly if that happens out of gratitude towards your father, who gave you life. Do not doubt!

When my prison sentence was extended for four years, I didn't hesitate for a second. This was the answer to my prayer. This was what Father Arsenie had told me in my dream. I took over the punishment that could be imposed on my father.

How can I not be forever grateful to Mother Theodosia (in the world, Zorica Lațcu) for having invited me to visit Father Arsenie. He was and remains a pillar for the Romanian

Orthodox Church, a brilliant Christian and an exemplary Romanian.

I got to know him when he experienced his heyday. He is rightly called 'the light of Transylvania' and in extrapolation 'the light of Romania'. He was not only light, but above all, flame. His eyes pierced through your entire person, his eyes saw your past, your present and your future, your talents and your mistakes. It was always an unquestionable experience of love, faith and wisdom. Also in his sternness, he was sweet and loving. It was a privilege to be corrected by a saint.

An excerpt from the book 'Părintele Arsenie Boca - un om mai presus de oameni' (Father Arsenie Boca, a person above the people), Publisher Agaton, Volume 4, 2011.

Father PETRU VAMVULESCU, Priest

Father Petru Vamvulescu (Sibiu) is a priest from Sibiu who visited Father Arsenie monthly during the 1970s. He met Father Arsenie at the age of 26. He was just married to Laura who, however, was not accepted by Petru's mother and therefore did not attend the wedding. The marriage of Petru and Laura was blessed with two children, Maria and Gabriel. Father Petru retired few years ago. He now lives as a hermit.

My father died when I was eleven years old. From that moment on, my mother, to whom I am very grateful, raised me. I was immensely sad when she could not accept my fiancé Laura and refused to attend the wedding. I often retired to the chapel of the Theological Faculty in Sibiu to pray to the Mother of God. A friend advised me to submit my problem to Father Arsenie who was painting the church in Drăgănescu. I vividly remembered our first meeting.

Father Arsenie was standing on the scaffolding in the altar room when I entered the church. He immediately stopped working and shouted: "Welcome, Petru!" How was that even possible?

He called me by my name although I never met him before nor did I inform anyone about our meeting. When I looked at him, I saw how two narrow strings of fire from his dark glasses were looking into my eyes. "Why are you shocked, Petru? My eyes are just like yours", Father Arsenie remarked.

He read my thoughts and my fears, then took off his glasses with a smile. These rays, which I clearly saw, disappeared. Did I witness the Light of the Transfiguration, which also flowed through the church of the Holy Grail during Easter night? Anyway, I told Father Arsenie about the very tense situation with my mother. He advised me to invite her to my deacon ordination and promised that he would pray for us and that everything would be fine. That also happened. My mother came to my deacon ordination. Her tears of anger and sorrow at my marriage with Laura turned into a source of relief and deep joy at my deacon ordination.

Laura died in 2004. After a debilitating battle that lasted twenty years, she lost the fight against the disease, which continuously attacked and exhausted her body – cancer. Father Arsenie always comforted and strengthened her with these wise words: "Let us not be angry with God when he calls us. Let us go more often to the Liturgy to receive Communion. We must learn (accept) that we are now already living in Heaven, that our life is just a wait for the inviting call from Above to meet Him, Him who was willing to be tortured and crucified and raised from the dead, for our salvation. He takes care of everyone, those who go and those who stay behind. We must continue to hope and believe in God and His Assistance, even after death."

It is precisely these words that have comforted and strengthened me when my daughter Maria died in an accident in 2005 at the age of 34. She was married to a priest and was the mother of three children.

Laura and Maria wonderfully found their final resting place among the graves with the nuns in Prislop. Their bodies were laid to rest until the day of their resurrection close to the grave of Father Arsenie who told us to faithfully attend the Divine Liturgy. "Despite everything, we must continue to give preference to the Divine Liturgy. Our prayers to Christ, the Mother of God and all Saints and the Divine Liturgy ensure that the world is not lost and that the Divine Spirit continues to give us life."

An excerpt from the newspaper article 'Petru Vanvulescu: Părintele Arsenie nu-i departe nici astăzi de cei ce îl cheamă în ajutor si uneori vine în taină, nevăzut de cei mulți' (Petru Vamvulescu: Father Arsenie is not far away today from those who call his help and sometimes comes in mystery, unseen by many) in the 'Sibiu 10%' newspaper, 3 April 2015.

IRINEU DUVLEA
Former Bishop of the Romanian-Orthodox Church in America (ROEA)

Father Irineu was born on 19 April 1962 in Alba Iulia (Romania). From 1993 until 2000, he was an archimandrite (abbot) of the Sâmbăta de Sus monastery. On 2 November 2002, he was ordained bishop of the Romanian Orthodox Church in the United States of America (ROEA) at Saint George Cathedral in Detroit. He continued to hold this position until 2017.

I first met Father Arsenie in the monastery at Sâmbăta de Sus during the autumn of 1980. I just entered as a brother. In secret, he visited the monastery with the nun Zamfira. Both wearing civilian clothes, they were still being shadowed by the Security Forces. Father Arsenie had grey hair and a short beard, but his gaze was deep and clear. I was working at the bakery of the monastery when Father Serafim Popescu informed us that Father Arsenie had arrived. Because I was told that Father Arsenie was clairvoyant, I initially did not want to meet him. I was really scared, but because Father Calinic Morar encouraged me and led me to Father Arsenie to receive his blessing, I dared and could not refuse. When Father Seraphim introduced me to

Father Arsenie as 'his disciple', he looked at me penetratingly and said: "Faith can move mountains, but let's see how he can move a mountain if his faith is put to the test." I think that was his last visit to the monastery. At least, I never heard that he visited the monastery afterwards.

Sometime later, Father Veniamin Tohăneanu, the abbot of the monastery, suggested me to become a monk. However, I felt extremely insecure. I did not, as I could not even dare, to make a decision. Many advised me to ask Father Arsenie for advice. I took the train to Bucharest and arrived around seven in the morning in Drăgănescu where Father Arsenie was working in the church. It was still dark when I entered the church. There was only light in the altar where Father Arsenie was painting. I was scared. What should I do or say?

-Who is there? And what do you want? What are you looking for here?
- Father Arsenie, Father Veniamin, the abbot of the monastery in Sâmbăta de Sus, wants me to become a monk. Should I do that? I don't know if that's good for me? Whether I am suitable?
- Do it. However, I will tell you one thing: finish your school and stick to your monastic vows, poverty, obedience and chastity. If you follow this, you will achieve perfection...
- You know, Father, I would like to become a deacon...
- You will receive a higher ordination than deacon. You

will serve the Church and your land on another shore over the great waters. Stay tolerant and patient in seeing human helplessness.

Initially, I did not understand these last few sentences until I was transferred to the United States to serve and lead the Romanian Church after twenty years of service as a monk in the monastery of Sâmbăta de Sus. Father Arsenie was able to foresee my future! He was able to see my destiny. I must confess humbly that I never met such a person again.

Of course, we also talked about other things during this meeting, but what I remember is the end of the conversation. Father Arsenie asked me then: "You also brought something from Sâmbăta de Sus?" I did indeed have some walnuts and honey with me. "Take them to the rectory, across the street. Give them to Mrs. Bunescu, the wife of the priest..." I left the church, crossed the street, and knocked on the gate of the rectory. As no one answered, I entered the garden where two menacing dogs were growling. They looked at me threateningly, but I passed by them and walked to the door. When the woman saw me, she was amazingly shocked. "How did you enter without being attacked? That never happens!" I answered that Father Arsenie had sent me to hand over the walnuts and honey. The woman looked at me surprised. I handed over the package and left. The moment I closed the gate behind me, the two dogs started barking loudly and jumping up against the fence. I was troubled when I came back into the church. Father Arsenie laughed when he asked me: "Shocked? That was a lesson in obedience! He who is obedient has nothing to fear. Also no watchdogs in a garden." I understood that Father Arsenie had the power to understand and influence the behavior of animals.

I was lucky enough to meet Father Arsenie again in the church of Drăgănescu, together with Father Timotei and Father Calinic. I spoke to him one last time, sometime in 1984, at the house of the brother of nun Mother Zamfira, located in the Aviator Iliescustreet in Bucharest. After that, Father Arsenie had problems with his health and withdrew into his cell from the monastic establishment in Sinaia. In November 1989, I was at the Ghighiu monastery where I attended the funeral of Father Gherman. There I felt the inner compulsion to go home earlier than planned. Via Brașov and Făgăraș, I returned by car to the monastery of Sâmbăta de Sus where I heard that Father Arsenie had died. Father Veniamin had already left for the monastery in Prislop where Father Arsenie was to be buried. Fortunately, I found another driver who could take me to Prislop where I could read Psalms[1] and pray at night for Father Arsenie. When everyone was getting ready for the funeral service, I was asked to carry the wooden cross, which is still on Father Arsenie's grave today. I felt unworthy for this.

---

1 It is customary in the Orthodox Church to read the Psalter continuously while standing before the body of the deceased during the vigil prior to the funeral service.

Mother Filoteia, a nun from the Prislop monastery, entrusted me with a whisper: "Father Irineu, now you carry the cross of Father Arsenie, but you will also have to carry it later..." I did not understand her words, but the true meaning only became clear to me after I had left Sâmbăta de Sus and received a new calling and mission in the United States.

I often think back to that exceptional time. With my fellow brothers, I am and prove to be grateful for the extraordinary blessing, which we experienced by getting to know Father Arsenie. Even though everyone goes his or her own way, God's Providence brings us to many unsuspected places or in unexpected circumstances. Those who know Father Arsenie know that he has a permanent hold. His life lessons in word and deed have given us light and love at the time, and they still do so today.

I still remember well the words that he often said to his visitors: "All my life I have tried to change people, but I have often not succeeded." What should I say then? I comfort others and myself with another one-liner from Father Arsenie: "God loves the greatest sinner more than the most beloved saint can ever love God." It is a comforting thought that makes me look forward to that moment when I will notice that God Himself is on the lookout to welcome me Home. It is the core message of the parable of 'The Prodigal Son'. No matter how far a person is from God and goes "into a distant land" (Luke 15: 13) to finally

"fill his belly with the skins that the pigs ate" (Luke 15: 16),
God is waiting for us. He waits for us, runs into us, hugs us and
gives us a new dress, a ring, new shoes and a welcome party. It
cannot be better said. Man can turn his back on God, but God
will never forget man, or as David sings in Psalm 103:

> The LORD is merciful and gracious,
> slow to anger and abounding in steadfast love.
> He will not always chide,
> nor will he keep his anger forever.
> He does not deal with us according to our sins,
> nor repay us according to our iniquities.
> For as high as the heavens are above the earth,
> so great is his steadfast love toward those who fear him;
> as far as the east is from the west,
> so far does he remove our transgressions from us.
> As a father shows compassion to his children,
> so the LORD shows compassion to those who fear him.
> (Psalm 103.8-13[2])

I am convinced that Father Arsenie has not left us. In fact,
he remains connected with us and lives with us in an unseen
and mystical way. May the Lord give him his earned rest and
give him an eternal memory. May we remember him and
commemorate him as a God-given guide on our path of life.

---

2 French version of the Septuagint Psalter by Father Placide [Deseille] of blessed memory.

This testimony was published in the book 'Părintele Arsenie Boca, Sfântul Ardealului' (Father Arsenie Boca, the Saint of Transylvania), Publisher Agnos, 2012.

Father IOAN PEANĂ
Priest

Ioan Peană is a retired priest in Gura Râului, the village where the church doors are never closed and the locals wear traditional Romanian clothes on public holidays. After his studies at the Theological Faculty in Sibiu, he was ordained a priest in Orlat in 1975. He became a chauffeur and confidant of Metropolitan (bishop) Nicolae Mladin, who in turn introduced him to Father Arsenie Boca, with whom he became and remained close friends.

I first met Father Boca in 1976. At the time, he still lived in Bucharest. Because he had been a political prisoner, he no longer had the right to work as a priest or to dress as a cleric. He then worked as a painter of icons and frescoes in the Church of Drăgănescu, and travelled back and forth on a daily basis. I accompanied Metropolitan Nicolae when he visited Father Arsenie at the request of Father Nicodim Zaharia. Father Nicodim was the confessor of Father Arsenie and is in fact buried next to him in the Monastery in Prislop. Father Arsenie and I became friends for life since then. I continued to visit him, even after the death of Metropolitan Nicolae, often in Drăgănescu, but mostly in Bucharest at his home. Almost nobody came there. Father Arsenie went to the church where he also met up with believers who wanted to see him. Telephone lines were still eavesdropped during those days.

Father Arsenie was very modest and rarely spoke about the past even though we often had very serious conversations. Every home visit, I brought milk and wine, and bread from the countryside. That made Father Arsenie very happy. In 1989 he retired, sick and debilitated, to Sinaia, where I was unable to visit him. During my last visit, he told me about his forthcoming demise. I know that many stories are circulating about his death, but they are all speculations. Only God knows how Father Arsenie died. His last words at the farewell in Bucharest were: "Be a good person. Take care of the parish and the believers!"

I do not visit Father Arsenie's last resting place in Prislop very often even though wonderful things happen there. For me, one must always visit a holy place with humility, not with a list full of wishes. Whoever does the latter acts out of self-interest such that visiting the dead becomes the goal and the means to get something out of it. That is not right, I think. The final resting place of Father Arsenie is a place where we can find the spirit of Father Arsenie and humbly entrust our earthly concerns and problems in faith to Christ and His Saints.

Father Arsenie was inexorably strict with sin and injustice, however mild and forgiving he was to the sinner and unjust. That is why the system found him to be an obstacle, and why he was subsequently prosecuted and locked up in prison. He always mentioned things by name, fearless and straightforward, but never judgmental. One day, with a number of parishioners from Orlat, I visited Father Arsenie in Drăgănescu. I informed him of this and asked for his permission, as I did not want to disturb him during his painting work nor did I want to mess with his schedule. I planned this visit to give some courage and comfort to the believers who all lived in families with issues. Alcoholism and debauchery were serious problems even during those days. When we entered the church, Father Arsenie came to us. He stopped at a woman and told her personally and in silence that she was the cause of her husband's alcoholism. The lady in question was shocked and thought that I had talked to Father Boca about her situation. Nothing could be further from the truth! Father Arsenie was able to see through every person, man or woman, boy or girl. Out of love for them, he confronted them with their sins, not to burden their conscience, but to ease their burden. Only those who recognize a problem can work on a solution. Those who do not know they are sick are not looking for a cure. By speaking about their sins, he gave them a chance for repentance, conversion, and deliverance. He did not make them prisoners. He gave them freedom.

Father Arsenie did not talk much. He was very silent. Occasionally, he told something about his mother Creștina, but never about himself. For example, I often travelled with Father Arsenie through Tram 12 to Şoseaua Alexandriei. Nothing was said along the way. He asked me to sit down while he kept standing although there were still seats available. He held onto a pole and stared at a spot outside. Did he meditate? Did he pray? He seemed to be in conversation with the Invisible Companion. Later, I found out that Metropolitan Nicolae prayed the same way. I started a conversation to make the trip more pleasant, but he kept staring silently through the window. When I asked him what he was doing, he replied: "You must teach Our Father to pray in supreme concentration within an hour!" I looked at him incomprehensibly. "Within an hour? It only took a minute at most!" "Exactly, but how do you pray? You say a few sentences that you have learned from the outside, but is that praying? No. You must say every sentence consciously, loudly or silently. However, you also must consciously ask yourself what the words mean. 'Our Father...' Us? Who are we? All of us? All who live now and also those who have already died or still have to be born! You understand? You have to concentrate on every word you speak and you can make a prayer on your own. That's how I pray..." I suspect Father Arsenie was praying in Tram 12 that way as though he were in a different world and not even aware that he was standing upright in a tram on his way to the final stop of Tram 12.

Father Arsenie died on 28 November 1989. I was present at the funeral. I remember that it was a sober, but peaceful and intimate service. His face glowed as if it were in deep peace, an expression of heavenly happiness – peace at last. A month later, the Revolution broke out. I am terribly sorry about one thing. Father Arsenie entrusted me with so many things I was unable to write them down nor remember them. Maybe, who knows? God will not allow me to do that anymore and therefore, must I have forgotten it?

This is an adaptation of the interview, which was conducted by Eveline Pāuna and published in the newspaper "Taifasuri", No. 655, 23-29 November 2017.

SIMION TODORAN
Priest-Professor

Simion Todoran is a former student of Father Arsenie Boca. He is a priest and professor of the New Testament at the Theological Faculty in Alba Julia. He is a member of the committee that examines the canonization of Father Arsenie. Together with Mother Zamfira, he has compiled the book "The Path To The Kingdom", which collates numerous texts from Father Arsenie.

My first meeting with Father Arsenie made a deep impression on me. With a group of young people and students from Făgăraş, I travelled to Drăgănescu with the blessing of my spiritual father, the current metropolitan, during my fourth year of theology as I had heard about a wonderful monk, a man, who could 'see' through his visitors and even gave them unsolicited advice. At the church in Drăgănescu, I saw Father Arsenie for the first time. I wanted to ask him if I should get married or go in a different direction with my life. However, even before I could ask him my question, he replied: "*She's good!*" Then he turned to my then girlfriend, now my wife: "*If only he wants to take you as his wife*". That was it! I followed Father Arsenie's advice.

Now, while reading the texts of, or the stories about Father Arsenie, I still feel a gracious sensation, which I have literally experienced personally. That is not an imagination or fantasy, but a deeply experienced reality that still overwhelms and moves me. He often wore white clothes. On his head he had a white woollen cap. His voice was clear and his eyes penetrated your body and soul. He had something special, something attractive, that was a little frightening at the same time, because it was strange and mysterious. I was very excited when I had the same experience with Metropolitan Nicolae Corneanu in 1995 while preparing the first edition of "The Path To The Kingdom". Reading his text (and thereafter the other testimonies) confirmed my experience of Father Arsenie's influence on my life.

Father Arsenie was very personal and confidential in his dealings. He often gave life-changing advice, which I have always obeyed. For example, I had serious doubts about the path that I wanted to follow as a young adult. I wanted to follow theological studies in Bucharest, but the admission requirements were very strict. Moreover, the students from Sibiu were considered somewhat inferior. His answer, however, was reassuring: "*Go. You will be admitted!*" This is how it also went. I was admitted without any problem. During my PhD he advised me to visit Father Stăniloae who had moved to Bucharest. I could easily make contact through my friend Dumitrel who was a cousin of Father Stăniloae. This, too, appears now to be a life-changing event. Working together with Father Stăniloae was not only a blessing for my PhD. More importantly, I learned so much from him about the Holy Fathers and became motivated to study the Patericon and the Philokalia[1], for example. That was also what Father Arsenie had taught me: *"Read the biographies and lessons of the Holy Fathers because theology without the Holy Fathers is a dead theology!"*

I was friends with Father Arsenie. During my theological studies in Bucharest, I was always allowed to visit him in Prislop and Sinaia, but he also warned me: *"Our friendship will cost you dearly. You will get problems."* This prediction also came true. For example, I was selected to represent Romanian Orthodoxy as a young theologian at the Sixth Assembly of the World Council of Churches. I attended the preparatory meetings in Sibiu and Cluj, but I was not allowed to leave. Perhaps, my friendship with Father Arsenie had something to do with it. I regretted this cancellation, but I spent that period meaningfully by further developing my doctoral thesis. Then, when I had to defend my thesis, I lost my manuscript. I had to start all over again. Father Arsenie advised me to remain calm in all circumstances – *"In all circumstances, always. Understood? Even when my name burns...!"* At first, I did not

---

1 The Philokalia of the Neptic Fathers (1782) is a Greek collection of texts written from the 4th to the 15th century and it discusses the mental prayer or the Jesus Prayer. It was compiled by Nicodemus the Hagiorite and Macarius of Corinth.

understand what he wanted to tell me, but later it became very clear to me. Priests, even during the Mass, began to defame Father Arsenie: "That Boca is a fool. He is married, does not take life seriously anymore. What he does is a shame for the Church. He must feel ashamed of himself." I was enraged. I wanted to defend Father Arsenie and our friendship, but I also wanted to remain obedient and calm. I stayed silent and prayed in silence. I entrusted Father Arsenie with everything I had heard, what I had thought. He gave me a reassuring look and said: "*It's nothing. Be patient, God will help you!*"

One day, Patriarch Teoctist came to Alba Julia with a delegation. I visited him and told him that I no longer felt at home and that I wanted to return to Bucharest to work. My request was approved and I thanked God for His help. When I visited Father Arsenie and told him about my meeting with the patriarch, he said: "That is not good! Stay there!" "But, Father, I have a PhD in theology, I want to teach theology!" "You will teach theology, but not in Bucharest! Have patience and trust!"

I did not understand anything at all. I was greatly surprised when later in Alba Julia some lectures were organized and afterwards a theological faculty was built. Perhaps, the faculty at Alba Julia has less charisma than this one at Sibiu, but I can testify with gratitude and pride that people work with enthusiasm and ambition. Theology is and remains a necessity from the beginning and for all time. The words of Father Arsenie came to fruition.

I have known Father Arsenie for ten years. I can't really call myself his student, but his friend and confidant. I have always faithfully followed his advice and literally everything he told me became a reality. There is more. In 1983, I lived in an apartment in Bucharest. This apartment in the Șerban Vodă Street, No. 33 belonged to the Church of the Holy Spiridon. Father Arsenie moved in with me after completing his assignment in the church at Drăgănescu. When the church was consecrated, Father Arsenie was not invited. He was not allowed to attend the Mass where other believers were present. As a result, he stayed in the flat, while Mother Maria and other nuns travelled to Drăgănescu to attend the festive ceremony. When they returned and told what they had experienced, it seemed that Father Arsenie could tell better than the sisters what had happened and how everything went. Isn't it surprising that Father Arsenie painted the martyr Stephen the New[2] in the altar of the church of Drăgănescu? Stephen the New is commemorated every November 28, the death anniversary of Father Arsenie. Coincidence? Foreknowledge? Intuition? I really know that God works through people and certainly through Father Arsenie even now, decades after his death.

---

2 Saint Stephen the New is a monk, defender of the icons, who was martyred during the iconoclastic persecution, under Constantine V Copronymus. It is remarkable that Father Arsenie's birth in Heaven took place on the feast day of this saint. Several learnings of Father Arsenie are taken from Philokalia (which he helped translate together with his spiritual superior, Father Dumitru Stăniloae), preaching the attainment of spiritual perfection by the stages of elevation of the soul defined in Philosophy.

I suspect that I was one of the last people to see Father Arsenie alive. Mother Zamfira, who did not allow anybody to see Father Arsenie, had left for Bucharest. I came to visit Father Arsenie that day. We talked a lot and had in-depth discussions until Mother Zamfira returned. When I said goodbye, he looked intently at me: "*We will not see each other again until we meet in the Kingdom of God...*"

I replied: "But, Father, I need you now. We cannot miss you here, you are indispensable to us!" What he then answered to me is unforgettable and extremely efficient: "*From where I am going, I can help you even more. Do not forget that!*"

They were his last words to me – words of comfort and encouragement that have always protected and guided me. Every time I wanted to go to Prislop or Sinaia, I have never encountered any obstacle, quite the contrary. In general, I cannot say that Father Arsenie ever got me into trouble or caused me pain or sorrow. I may have made him disappointed, angry, scared, or sad due to my behavior and ignorance. I was not at his spiritual level. I was not as serious as he was. I did not do as much work as he did. I did not worship God as much as he did.

I saw Father Arsenie not only when he was still alive, but also when he was laid to rest after his death. It was beautiful, with a serene face that I could remember months later. He had the face of a saint. "*Father Arsenie, you were great during your life.*

You will remain great during your death and after your death."
With these words, I thanked him.

Father Arsenie was wonderfully exceptional. He had an extraordinary spirit who knew how to live in a God-pleasing way and how to prepare for death. Doubtless, that is why pilgrims go to Prislop. They want to continue to meet the spirit of Father Arsenie. Pilgrims do not go there by invitation, or because there is a special service, or to witness a miracle. They go there because they love Father Arsenie. That is why I am convinced that God will do His work and pay tribute to Father Arsenie, His servant.

Father Arsenie acted humbly and unobtrusively. He definitely did not want to stand out. When he lived in my house, he took care of our four-year old girls when I had to work. He played with them and fed them. He was really good with them and they enjoyed his company. He also rejected any preferential treatment at the table. When I wanted to give him some more food, he immediately rejected it: "I eat as much as you do. No more!" His bed was also too short. He was quite tall, about 1.8 m. His feet stuck out at the end when lay in bed. I was ashamed and wondered what to do, but he read my mind and strongly forbade me to do anything.

Remarkable it was that he liked reading so often, especially about anthropology and dogmatism. He wondered why it was that the large family, in which Basil the Great grew up, produced so many bishops, monks and nuns. Six saints decorated the calendar! "How did they live? How can they serve as an example for the people of today?" Father Arsenie was a serious man, his life's goal was to serve God. Everything was planned, he did nothing cautiously. He lived very involved. He investigated, watched, and listened carefully.

Father Teofil described Father Arsenie as a spiritual genius and exceptional. Father Bodogae said: "Father Arsenie Boca was sensational. He would appear and disappear." Professor Ică told me that during a meeting in 1970, Father Arsenie had "appeared and disappeared." Appear and disappear – how can we understand these words? How can we explain such an event? Let me entrust this fact to you in all sincerity. I was in Alba Julia when I also saw Father Arsenie, at least for a few moments. He was then without a trace. I thought I was wrong. When I saw him a few days later in Sinaia, I asked him if he had been to Alba Julia. He replied: "Indeed, I was there."

Father Arsenie fasted and prayed. He did exceptional and wonderful things – things that we, too, can do if we live in the same way as Father Arsenie so that we receive the gift and grace from God to accomplish such things. That is really not possible if you only live for yourself and not for your neighbor.

Let us remember Father Arsenie in a serious and serene way. Let us follow his advice such as, for example, this advice, with which I conclude this plea: "*You must protect your head against two things – against the cold and against foolishness.*"

Amen.

This speech was held at the Centenary of the birth of Father Arsenie Boca at the Brâncoveanu Monastery in Sâmbăta de Sus on Saturday, 25 September 2010 and was subsequently published in the book "Părintele Arsenie Boca, un om mai presus de oameni" (Father Arsenie Boca, a man exalted above men), Publisher Agaton, Volume 4, 2011.

DANIIL
STOENESCU
Former Bishop of Dacia Felix

Bishop Daniil Stoenescu was born on 23 September 1957 in Hățăgel. He graduated from the Theological Faculty in Sibiu and obtained the title of 'Doctor of Theology' from the Orthodox Theological Institute in Bucharest and the University of Thessaloniki (Greece). He was a monk in the monasteries of Hodoș-Bodrog, Prislop and Densus-Hunedoara. As a disciple of Father Arsenie, he wrote many publications about the life, writings and icons of Romania's most beloved monk.

"Lord God, Who lives mysteriously among people, have compassion on us and be merciful to us!" These are the familiar opening words of Father Arsenie's prayer, which I remembered during the homily of His Eminence Metropolitan Laurențiu, held on that day and on that place, where we are united to be able to meet Christ among us, together with Father Arsenie. "God, Who lives mysteriously among people, have compassion on us and be merciful to us!" This being together is not an exclusive, scientific symposium. It is not even a theological symposium. It is a meeting of soul mates who testify about their experiences with Father Arsenie Boca during his life and yes, even after his death. I, too, had the unspeakable pleasure of getting to know Father Arsenie. It is again a great joy for me today to share this pleasure with you all.

I try to do this, with your approval, based on a number of metaphors. 'Metaphor' is the word I read on Greek trucks when I was studying in Thessaloniki. Metaphor means 'transportation'. A metaphor is also a figure of speech, that takes us to a second plane, a different time, or a different place, where the subject (the Orthodox Faith and the Canonization of Father Arsenie Boca) is explained and interpreted in a different and better way.

I first met Father Arsenie during the feast of Saint Demetrius in the church of Drăgănescu in 1979. He looked at me intently. His first words to me were: "Study the scriptures from the Philokalia and read the stories from the Patericon[1]." I also used the same words as a motto in my PhD thesis, which was about the theology of the Desert Fathers. The Egyptian Patericon is a basic work for our orthodox spirituality. It is a required reading for all monks and a recommended book for all Christians. The book is a collection of events, lessons, miracles and visions from the life of the Egyptian Desert Fathers.

---

1 Spiritual book containing saints and pious anecdotes about them. Orthodox countries and their large monasteries generally have a Patéricon, which mentions the Fathers who illustrated it. Contemporary Romanian Patéricon online:https://www.vies-consacrees.be/IMG/pdf/fzez_2008-2_dragoi.pdf

A clairvoyant monk tells how he sees Saint Arsenius the Great in a vision and whose name bore Father Arsenie with much respect and dignity. He saw the saint, surrounded by God's Spirit, floating above the water. Arsenius the Great lived during the fourth century and was a contemporary of Saint Anthony the Great and Saint Macarius the Great. He gave lessons to the sons of King Theodosius the Great and became a monk in Egypt. In my book 'Archangel of Prislop,' a 300-page book about Father Arsenie, I interpreted this vision of Holy Arsenius the Great. I did not let Father Arsenie Boca float on the water. He was not alone either. Father Arsenie was on a ship, the ship of the Romanian Orthodox Church. Numerous saints surrounded him and God's Spirit and Grace protected all. The Ship of Christ crossed all waters of the world until the end of days. Father Arsenie was never alone, not even during the lonely hours of prayer and reading. He felt surrounded by his examples, the saints.

I see Father Arsenie Boca today as the Moses of our nation. He was Elijah the Prophet for this land. Like a contemporary Apostle Paul, he testified about Christ to his countrymen. He was a modern-day John Chrysostom for Romania who with his fiery words, was able to ignite and flare up the faith in the hearts of listeners. What Mount Sinai was to Moses, Mount Athos was to Father Arsenie who lived there for four months. When I compiled the book 'The man dressed in linen, an angel with a golden censer' with unpublished texts from Father

Arsenie, I found his travel pass, which allowed him to leave Romania via Stamora Moravița, Vârșeț and Belgrade to travel back and forth to Mount Athos, in the years 1938-1939. I was very happy with this discovery, especially when I later travelled along the same route to Greece. I derived the title of this book from quotes from the books of Ezekiel and Revelation.

Why do I compare Father Arsenie with Prophet Elijah? What the Carmel was for the Prophet Elijah, for Father Arsenie those were the altars of the monastery churches in Sâmbăta and in Prislop and of the church in Drăgănescu. There, during the Liturgy, he descended from the Fire of Heaven in an unknown and unseen way on the Bloodless Sacrifice. What Mount Horeb (Sinai) was to Elijah, to Father Arsenie, was his cell in the mountains of Făgăraș, near Sâmbăta.

Why do I call Father Arsenie 'a contemporary Apostle Paul?' Apostle Paul was mocked and silenced when he testified before the Greeks on the Areopagus in Athens about their 'Unknown God' (Acts 17). He left Athens and travelled on to Corinth. Father Arsenie was also silenced in May 1959. Communists forbade him access to the monastery. Father Arsenie has entrusted that to me.

Why do I call Father Arsenie 'a contemporary John Chrysostom?' Saint John Chrysostom was a priest in Antioch and later became archbishop in Constantinople. He died in exile. Similarly, Father Arsenie was a hieromonk[2] and abbot here in the Sâmbăta Monastery during the years 1939-1948. On 15 November 1948, Father Arsenie moved, at the request of Metropolitan Bălan, from Sâmbăta to Prislop where he resided until 1959. Whereas John Chrysostom travelled from Antioch to Constantinople, Father Arsenie traversed Sâmbăta to Prislop. John Chrysostom was wrongly convicted and sent into exile at the Council of 403 where he died. Father Arsenie also died as an exile, banished. After working in the studio of the Romanian Patriarchate for several years, under the greatest possible protection of Patriarch Justinian, Father Arsenie worked for 15 years as an icon and fresco painter in the church of Drăgănescu. He spent his last 15 years in the Monastic establishment where to this day his hand-built house and his monastic mountain vault are being honored. John Chrysostom was rehabilitated and later also declared a saint. That is what Father Arsenie is also awaiting for. He will be rehabilitated and declared a saint. That is beyond doubt. People may regret or like it, promote or try to prevent it, but it will happen! Why? Because Father Arsenie is an exceptional personality in all his simplicity and sincerity. He is prophetic, apostolic and patristic. These are the characteristics referring to figures from the Bible: the prophets, the apostles and the forefathers.

This year, the Serbian Orthodox Church has rightly declared Father Justin Popovitch a saint. However, his grave does not

2 Monk-priest.

even count one thousandth of the number of visitors that visited the place where Father Arsenie is buried. People from all ranks and walks of life in our society love Father Arsenie and appeal to his help and assistance. During the 20th anniversary of the death of Father Arsenie, on Saturday, 28 November 2009, according to police estimates, about 40.000 pilgrims visited the Prislop Monastery. For the entire weekend, from Friday morning to Sunday night, the number of visitors was estimated at 90.000.

The spiritual legacy of Father Arsenie is unprecedentedly large and he is loved by so many people. First of all there is the book 'The Path to the Kingdom', a collection of texts that were written here, in the Sâmbăta Monastery. I published the homilies, which Father Arsenie held in Prislop until 1952, under the title 'Living Words'. 'The Romanian Orthodox Sistine Chapel' is the title of the book describing Father Arsenie's work for the church of Drăgănescu. I was asked to write a preface for this publication, which contains around 350 pages of previously unpublished texts. All the texts of the speeches, which I held for 20 years at the commemorative parties of 8 May and 28 November, were collected and published under the title 'The Angel of Prislop'. This book also has no less than 300 pages. It is very clear to me. I like to talk and write a lot about Father Arsenie – too much, perhaps. The spiritual legacy is therefore very extensive, exceptional and unique. No one can accuse me of any kind of exaggeration if today I repeat the words I uttered during Father Arsenie's funeral: "Apostle Andreas, the first called, was also named an Apostle of Romania, as he was the first one to bring the Gospel to our country. I do not think that, apart from Apostle Andreas, someone with the same spiritual gift and drive as Father Arsenie has blessed our country through his life, in word and deed." With the words from an interview that was broadcasted on Romanian TV, I was able to testify about Father Boca: "Father Arsenie is a Mount Everest for the Romanian people."

Father Arsenie lived like a saint, humble and obedient. He has never sought his personal followers that have flooded our country in the past decades, but the following around Father Arsenie is the result of his exceptionally true lifestyle, imbued with Christ. "The deep, warm heart of every human being cannot but love Christ." This statement by Father Arsenie is visibly confirmed by the many thousands of pilgrims who visit Prislop to rediscover the authenticity and truth of the Orthodox Faith in the publications by and about Father Arsenie. They are drenched with the Living Water from the Divine Source, which continues to refresh and cleanse permanently. I do not believe that the following of Father Arsenie will soon decrease. It is such a unique phenomenon that impresses the entire Orthodox world and immediately challenges every believer: "What is my responsibility in such an event? How do I stand as a Christian in this everyday world? To what extent do I dare to take Father Arsenie as an example and as a guide?" These are the questions that Father Arsenie would undoubtedly ask all members of the Church, hierarchs and theologians, the clergy and particularly those at the monastery in Prislop.

In 1990, I wrote a short article for the magazine 'The Thinking' which, however, could not appear due to the death of Mother Zamfira. I then wrote about the day that Father Arsenie died: "Today, November 28, is a day with the Cross. Yes, even a day with the Red Cross, which is set up and displayed at the Sinai height of Sâmbăta and which also flaunts on Mount Carmel of Prislop, on Mount Tabor of Drăgănescu and on the top of Mount of Olives in Sinaia." Today, in 2010, I see Father Arsenie standing on Mount Tabor of our Romanian nation in the company of the Glorified Christ, with Moses and Elijah, with Peter, James and John and with all the saints of our country. I see him as a Saint among the Saints, before Jesus Christ, the Saint of the Saints, as the prophet Daniel calls him and praises him. I see Father Arsenie holding out his saving hand to the sinking Romania, which threatens to sink into the whirlpools of our time, as Christ held out His hand to pull Peter up from the heavy waves of storm. Christ still does that, always and everywhere, in and through His Saints. I truly believe that this modern age would be even harder, darker and more threatening and that the storm would last longer without our cries for help and without the prayers of the Saints. I am convinced that the spiritual legacy of Father Arsenie offers salvation in this time of storm and thunder.

I see Father Arsenie walking with us and among us. He is with Christ, with us and with our country on his way to Emmaus. There shall we, Jesus' followers, recognize and acknowledge Christ, just as Father Arsenie did.

Last night, I was exceptionally surprised and very excited when I noticed that in the new Orthodox Cathedral of Făgăraş, hundreds of people were waiting for us with a piece of clothing that Father Arsenie once wore for a very long time. I suspected that there were only three similar ones. The first hangs in his cell in Sinaia, the second was a gift from Mother Zamfira and hangs in my old cell in my home village and the third is in a coffin in the cathedral of Făgăraş.

That is beautiful and good. It reminds me of the vision of Father Arsenius the Great from the fourth century. His contemporary, Father Hilarion the Great, established monasticism in Palestine. Hilarion was friends with Bishop Epiphanius of Salamis in Cyprus, who himself was ordained a monk by Hilarion in his Palestinian monastery and invited him to travel from Palestine to Cyprus and to help the Christian Faith to take root and flourish. Hilarion accepted the invitation and the challenge, succeeded more than convincingly in his venture and thereafter travelled back to his monastery in Palestine. At his death, the people of Palestine cheered: "We have his body, his bones and his relics." The Cypriots also sang out: "We have his spirit."

Father Arsenie's body is buried in Prislop. His spirit carries on in Prislop, but also here, in Sâmbăta, in Drăgănescu, in Sinaia and in many other places – maybe also, hopefully, in your town or city, even in your home. Even more than his garments and his body, we must focus on the spirit of Father Arsenie. Today, at the centenary of the birth of Father Arsenie, we have been invited and called to seek the spirit of Father Arsenie under the ashes of the past. We will find and rediscover his spirit in the smouldering grace of the Mass, in the liberating sacrament of confession, in the thunder of the homily, and in the lightning of the Divine Providence. This year it is exactly 62 years ago that Father Arsenie left Sâmbăta and this first symposium looks like a return of Father Arsenie to Sâmbăta. I don't think it is. After all, how can someone return to a place he has never left? This is where the spirit of Father Arsenie lives, whose body is buried in an oak coffin in Prislop. Father Arsenie has always obeyed the decision of the Romanian Orthodox Church. That will be no different with the upcoming decision regarding his possible canonization when the Synod will make known God's Will.

Today, we celebrate Father Arsenie's centenary. Yesterday, while I was on my way from Ţara Haţegului to Făgăras, I realized that history was rolling down the centuries. History does not take centenaries into account. The centenary of the birth of Mihai Eminescu (1850-1889)[3] fell during the most complex

---

3 Romania's most famous romantic poet, whose works have been translated into more than 60 languages. He is also considered by the historian Nicolae Iorga (1871-1940) as the god-father of the modern Romanian language.

period in recent Romanian history. While celebrating the centenary of the birth of Saint Simeon the New Theologian, the Roman Catholic Church separated from the Orthodox Church, but at the centenary of Saint Maximus the Confessor, the Sixth Ecumenical Council fortunately took place in Constantinople (680-681). The centenary celebrations of Saint John Chrysostom and of blessed Augustine coincided with the Fourth Ecumenical Council in Chalcedon. On the centenary of Saint Basil the Great, the Third Ecumenical Council took place in Ephesus. During the preparations for the centenary of the Saint Apostle Paul, Saint Ignatius of Antioch died in Rome. A hundred years after the birth of Jesus Christ, the God-man received the Saint Apostle and Evangelist John the mystery of Revelation[4].

I thank you all very much for your patience in listening and I thank the Archbishop and Metropolitan for their approval to be present here today and tomorrow at this Centenary and the Liturgy.

I see a rainbow between Sâmbăta and Prislop, a chain of gold between Făgăraș and Hațeg. May God bless us and Father Arsenie today and in all the days of our lives and may He continue to live with us and among us with the words that Father Arsenie taught us to pray: "Lord God, Who lives

---

4 And he transcribed it in the book of Revelation.

mysteriously among people, have mercy on us and be merciful to us!" Amen.

This lecture was given at the Centenary of the birth of Father Arsenie Boca in the Brâncoveanu Monastery in Sâmbăta de Sus, on Saturday, 25 September 2010 and was subsequently published in the book 'Părintele Arsenie Boca, un om mai presus de oameni' (Father Arsenie Boca, a person above the people), Publisher Agaton, Volume 4, 2011.

BOGDAN JUNCU
Spiritual Child of
Father Arsenie

Bogdan Juncu was a cheerful young man from Teleorman. He moved to Făgăraş where he got married and raised a happy family with a wife and two children. He likes to hunt and has a weapons license. When the stress at work becomes too much for him, he relaxes by wandering around, hunting in a nature for a day. During such a day off, his wife took the opportunity to leave the house with their two children, unannounced and without any reason. There was only a written note that she was 'fed up with life.' They never had arguments or fights. She took all the furniture with her. Bogdan was left alone, desperate and irrecoverable. Someone advised him to visit Father Arsenie. Later on, a monk addressed him in a nightly dream. His mother also advised him to visit Father Arsenie. It was the beginning of a long-standing, spiritual friendship – a spiritual bond between a father and a son.

I gave Father Arsenie a picture of my wife. He looked at the photo carefully for minutes. Then, he looked at me with his piercing blue eyes.

- What did she write to you? That she is tired of life? She is lying.

They are both lying, she and her mother. The moment will come when they will have to pay the toll. She will get sick, seriously ill. She will not have a happy life.

(Later, I learned that my ex-wife remarried twice. She was beaten by both of her men. She is not doing well.)

When he returned the photo to me, he warned me:

- Do not start drinking. Do not grab the bottle to drown your grief.
- Father, in principle, I don't drink.
- Principle or not, avoid the alcohol. Are you listening?

I still remember his words like I heard them only yesterday, his gaze too, which accompanied the warning. However, it was in vain. Two months after our first meeting, I started drinking, unsuspectingly. Initially, it was only one beer a day until one became two, three, four, then five. One morning in July 1983, I woke up refreshed. Not surprisingly, I had not (remarkably) drunk the previous day. Then, I heard his voice echoing through the house, more real than the voice of someone, directly addressing me.

- Boy! Boy! Boy!

I looked around me, but did not see anybody. This was not a drunken man's speech. I really heard Father Arsenie's voice and immediately knew what he meant. It was the same warning I heard from his mouth months ago during our first meeting. "Boy, stop drinking!" From that moment, I have not drunk a drop of alcohol – not on my birthday, not during Christmas or on New Year's Eve, not on Easter. Never again and that is not to my credit. Father Arsenie deserves the entire honor because it is he who protects and leads me. From that morning in July, I have changed my life. Not only did I stop drinking, but I also found joy during my free time in praying and reading books about saints, theological or Biblical subjects. I got to know God. No, not only from the books, but especially through experiencing His Grace and through everything that was granted to me. God's goodness really transcends all imagination. I would like to name a few examples of this, but I want to emphasize that this is not about me, but about what God gives through Father Arsenie to people who want to seek and follow His Path. (...)

One day I was staying with my mother. I was talking to her at the gate where a bus would pick me up at 1:30 pm and take me to work. It was a beautiful day. The sun was shining in the blue sky, and there was no cloud to be seen. During our chatter, I saw how a 'cloud or fog' formed in the sky, descended, positioned itself between the pillar at our house and the little linden tree, lingered there for a moment, ascended again and descended on the same spot, then ascended and descended again. I thought my eyes were blemished. I rubbed my eyes. A luminous figure with a radiant, fine face emerged from the mist. He was dressed simply and spoke to us with a soft voice.

- Don't you have a place for me to stay the night?
- No, not immediately, but maybe you can inquire from a hotel in the city?
- Mama, let him spend the night here. Our house is big enough, you can certainly free up a place for him...
- No, boy. You know how your father is...

I turned curiously to the radiant young man, who stared me right in the eye. A totally strange feeling overwhelmed me.

- Where do you come from?
- From afar.
- How far from here?
- Very far.

I know that his answer indicated that my question was purely rhetorical. He looked at me with a look that reminded me of my first meeting with Father Arsenie. How his light blue eyes suddenly turned black like night and a little later they again reflected a heavenly color.

- Mama, let him spend the night here.
- No, boy, we do not have enough space. And besides, Father

would...

The young man shook his head laughing as if he wanted to thank us for the effort. Then he took two steps, not a few. Two steps: one, two. Then, he disappeared from our view. I looked into the street, but there was nobody to be seen. My mother's face turned pale and probably mine too.

- Mom, that was not a person. That was...
- How can you say that, boy. Why are you talking like that?
- But, mom, look. Take a look. Where did he go?

I had to tell an outsider about this event. Somebody who tried to understand me. I looked for Father Teofil.

- Father, forgive me for disturbing you!
- Real friends never disturb. They talk to each other, they meet.
- Father, I'm afraid I'm going crazy.
- Crazy, Bogdan. Christians are not crazy, but wise. Tell me!

After telling him my story extensively, he took my hands and gently squeezed them. He looked at me comfortingly and confidently he said:

- Bogdan, Bogdan! You have no one to blame, not even your mother. The young man would not have stayed. He just wanted to test your goodwill, nothing more.

He did not tell me if this young man was an angel or a saint. I suspected it was Father Arsenie although I was not sure. It was a magnificent appearance, a beautiful figure.

My sister, Tuța, did not know much about Father Arsenie. I had advised her that in the event of an emergency to always beg Father Arsenie for help. One day, she travelled to Bucharest to visit her son who worked for the police. She took her grandson for a walk to Herăstrău Park where she suddenly became unwell. Her heart started beating very quickly, making it difficult for her to breath. She took her cell phone immediately to inform her son about her critical condition. He hurried to the park and called some friendly doctors along the way, including a cardiologist, who advised him to take his mother straight to the hospital where he treated all of his patients. He was able to immediately perform the most urgent actions. An electrocardiogram proved the seriousness of the situation. It is impossible for my sister to leave the hospital. She must remain in intensive care so that the doctors could continue to monitor her situation. The cardiologist left his desk to arrange a room for my sister. Tuța was left behind alone. She remembered my words and called on Father Arsenie.

- Father Arsenie, I have never known you and you will never know me. If what is told about you is true, I beg you to immediately give me back my health so that I can go home immediately. Heal me, Father Arsenie.

At that moment, the cardiologist entered his desk.

- Madam, I have good news. I found a room.
- Doctor, that is no longer necessary, I am healed.
- Madam, your situation is very serious. You must stay here the next few days. Don't worry, I've found a room and we'll take good care of you.
- But, doctor, I am healed, I feel good again.
- Madam, the electrocardiogram proves the seriousness of the situation. I have to insist that only rest...
- Doctor, I am healed.
- That is not possible!
- It's so!
- I will make a second electrocardiogram.

The cardiologist was extremely surprised when he saw the result. Nowhere was there a trace of the heart attack. My sister was completely healed. She did not mention a word about Father Arsenie, but everyone understood that a miracle had happened.

Another very remarkable story I heard came from the mouth of a 38-year-old man from Braşov. I got to know him when a number of people from the Agaton publishing house invited me to bring a large memorial cross to Father Arsenie's mountain cell in Sâmbăta de Sus.

- Mr Bogdan, I am 38 years old. I have never doubted the

existence of God, but I have enjoyed life since my youth. You know, the females and the drinking. Then, I heard about Father Arsenie. After reading two books about him, I decided to visit his grave in Prislop. Night fell when I arrived at the monastery cemetery. A man lit three candles on a bench near the grave. I stayed around a bit. After an hour and a half, I saw that two candles have already burned out extensively, while the third one seemed to have been lit just now. Two hours later, I noticed that the two candles were almost completely burned out, while the third candle did not get smaller. I couldn't believe my eyes. I sat down next to the man on the bench and asked him what happened. He answered me with a smile and told me that it happens to him every year! He asked me to stay with him until the morning because then, at 8 am exactly, the flame of the candle will go out. I stayed with him and witnessed exactly what he told me. At exactly 8 a.m., the flame of the candle extinguished, the length of which has remained unchanged all the entire time. I asked the man how that was possible. He answered me:

- Father Arsenie has helped me when I found myself in a problematic situation. Out of gratitude, I promised to light three candles every year here at his grave – one for him, one for my family, and one for my circle of friends. Every year, the candle for Father Arsenie keeps burning until eight in the morning. Then, the flame of the candle goes out, which has not become shorter after hours of burning.

- Mr Bogdan, I know this is physically impossible, but I have seen it myself. I myself would never have believed that story, but I was able to experience it myself. That is why I know that God exists and that there are holy people. A saint is buried in that grave in Prislop. This experience was the moment of my conversion. My life in debauchery is over. What I only wish is to find a good wife to start a family with. (...)

Father Bunescu entrusted the following story to me, a few months before his death. He was then 92 years old and had an extremely active memory, unlike his body, which had become weak. Father Arsenie worked in the church in Drăgănescu and was able to have lunch with the Bunescu family.

- Father Arsenie painted the interior of the Nicholas Church and came to eat with my wife and me. We had drawn up a strict arrangement. Father Arsenie liked discipline and followed our arrangement very rigorously. He never came too late, except for that one day when he didn't show up for the meal. I went looking where he was. The church door was open. Nobody was visible. I looked through the curtains of the Royal Doors[1] and saw Father Arsenie kneeling in front of the Altar, his head resting on his hands holding the edge

---

1 The Royal Doors or Holy Doors are the doors of the iconostasis [called Wall of icons in the Orthodox Church], which separate the sanctuary where the altar of the faithful is in the nave. It is a reminder of the veil of the Temple, which in the Old Covenant separated the Holy of Holies from the people.

of the Altar. I went back home and told my wife what I saw. When Father Arsenie came to the table a little later, he had tears in his eyes.

- Father Arsenie, what has happened?
- Never mind, Father. You will hear about it tomorrow morning.
- Father Arsenie, what happened? What will I hear tomorrow morning?
- I begged God not to let the Soviet troops invade our country.
- Who will invade our country, Father?
- The Soviet Union and their allies.
- Which allies?
- Father, you can hear about it tomorrow morning!

A day later, our country was flooded with national and international radio reporting, the Soviet army had invaded Czechoslovakia to defend the Bresjnev doctrine, along with the Warsaw Pact troops. Ceauşescu, himself a communist, warned our country about a Russian invasion. Black clouds gathered above Romania. Father Arsenie had foreseen this.

A lot can be told about Father Arsenie. This is also a special story. Father Panteleimon who was a priest in Ghighiu really wanted to attend the Holy Liturgy in Prislop. He had cherished Father Arsenie in his heart since he was a teenager and loved him with true, warm love. That is why he travelled one day from Ghighiu to Prislop. His driver and himself drove almost eight hours. (The total distance was about 450 km.) After the Divine Liturgy, the two of them returned home although they both had a feeling that a third person was in the back seat. Father Panteleimon told me that he himself had looked back several times. The feeling of an invisible presence did not let him go. He said:

- During the way back, our car didn't seem to hit the asphalt. We also didn't hear the engine roar. It seemed as if we were travelling in a timeless dream. Afterwards, the driver told me that he wanted to ask me if I also had the feeling that I was not alone, but he just kept silent because he was afraid to look ridiculous. I would probably come across ridiculous and unbelievable as well when I tell you that we were back in Ghighiu just after four hours of driving. When we arrived, the driver and I heard a voice telling us: "Till here, I have brought you. From here, you must go your own way."

Fragment from the book 'Părintele Arsenie Boca, Sfântul Ardealului' (Father Arsenie Boca, the Saint of Transylvania), Romeo Petraşciuc, p. 107-167, Publisher Agnos, 2012.

GEORGE VÂLCEA
Carpenter

George Vâlcea was the carpenter who made the grave cross of Father Arsenie. He worked together with Father Arsenie during the last twelve years of Father Arsenie's life. Not only did they become very close friends, but they were soulmates as well.

"If someone told me that I could meet Father Arsenie again here on earth by digging an immense tunnel towards him, I would not hesitate for a second and I would immediately start my assignment! That man has left this fire in my heart!"

(November 1989. Outside, a light layer of snow covers the earth. Small flakes stick to the windowpane and melt quickly. A warm sadness fills the work room, a chisel bites itself into the hard wood. Each tap of the hammer forms a piece of letter. George lets his hands glide over the first word, 'Arsenie.' Another nine letters await release from the wood: 'Hieromonk' or priest-monk. The "H" is long and slender and was designed by Father Arsenie himself, for whom the cross is intended. The short strokes that outline the edges are like the echo of the fast beating of his heart where sorrow rises. The tears arise almost immediately. The image becomes blurry. The chisel and the hammer are gently put on the worktable, while both hands are looking for a hold. Memories dig deep into the memory of the carpenter. The goodbye cannot be endured. "Come to my grave, George. Later I will be able to help you there better than I can do right now." They seem words from yesterday. "Goodbye, see you soon." Only now the emptiness yawns. So does the hopelessness.

George Vâlcea has become an old man. At almost the age of 80, he is still working at his work room in Comarnic. Here, between the boards, nails, hammers and chisels, he got to know Father Arsenie. He spent the last twelve years of his life with him, the best-known priest and most loved confessor from Transylvania.)

At that time I was still in the prime of my life. One day, a friend came to see me. He told me that he had an assignment for Sinaia. In Sinaia, for what?
He didn't know either, but I just had to sign up. I went and rang the doorbell at the house, the address of which I had received. It turned out to be inhabited by a number of nuns who had been banned from their monastery by the communists in 1959. I must admit that I was a bit scared of taking on the assignment. I could be prosecuted. However, the doubt faded away and I carried out the tasks that the sisters offered me on drawings. They were especially well executed and rather exceptionally detailed. They were almost little pieces of art. When I asked

the nuns where the sketches were coming from, they replied to me that an engineer had made them. "Impossible", I thought. I knew, without a doubt, that a talented artist could only have made these drawings, but I did not ask any further. I did the work for two years, exactly according to the drawings. The answer came naturally one day.

One day, I got a visit from a slender and distinguished, elderly gentleman in a tight civilian suit. He turned out to be Father Arsenie Boca, a monk who was also banned from his monastery and hidden from the outside world, living his life in complete anonymity and supreme simplicity. I still remember his piercing blue eyes and the first words he spoke to me. It seems as the day of yesterday. "Uncle Vâlcea, you don't know me, but I know you very well. From today onwards, you are part of our family." He knew my name although I had never met him before. Had he inquired about me? Interrogated people from my area? My suspicion quickly made way for shame: how could I ever question such a humble, honest and kind man? I have never met such a person, never will I meet such a man again. He didn't seem to be someone from this world. He was already a saint during his life.

That turned out some time later. I worked on the roof of the monastic establishment, while Father Arsenie watched carefully from the ground and gave me instructions. When I ended work tired that evening, I did not take the time to wish Father Arsenie a good evening. The next day, Father Arsenie was waiting for me with a cup of tea. After breakfast he got up, came to me and embraced me with the words: "Uncle Vâlcea, forgive me if I said or did something wrong yesterday. Forgive me everything and I will also forgive you everything and nothing can separate us. Nothing in this world and not in the next one!" I was surprised, but his words became reality. A friendship blossomed from this cordial embrace that transcended all boundaries of space and time. A kinship of souls, reaching deeper than the everyday being 'at peace': it touches the deeply experienced 'of being at peace.'

Father Arsenie often came to visit my work room during the last years of his earthly and anonymous life. We talked about everything, often I asked him all kinds of questions, about this life on earth and especially about the life beyond that awaits every person. He listened intently and answered carefully, as though he wanted to be absolutely certain that I understood him completely. Many claim he was a hard man. I have never experienced or have known him like that. On the contrary, he was always modest and very gentle. His character, just like his insight into people, life and the future, was extremely rare. **Wonderfully exceptional!**

That became apparent when my wife was examined by a team of specialists at the Parhon Hospital in Bucharest. She was not feeling well for quite some time. The diagnosis was inexorable:

a life-threatening cancer in an advanced stage. We were referred to the Philantropia hospital where the responsible doctor suggested surgery to us, not to save my wife's life, but to extend it by a few weeks or months at most. "The chance of success is extremely minimal, almost zero. If you believe in God, prayer may be a better solution. All help must come from Above." The message was clear, but incredibly difficult. It was like a hammer blow that destroyed my life within one second. Crying, I took the train to Sinaia where Father Arsenie was waiting for me peacefully. He told me about his life and about the work in the monastery in Prislop. He tried to distract my attention and offered me some distraction, but I kept thinking about my wife and the inexorable diagnosis. Father Arsenie was my only hope for my wife, my only partner with whom I spent my life. Together we had no children. I wanted to tell him about her illness, but he just kept talking. When my visit came to an end, he looked at me penetratingly, but comfortingly and said: "Uncle Vâlcea, do not worry. Let your wife be operated in Bucharest. Everything will be fine." I hadn't even had the chance to explain my problems and he gave me the advice that I was waiting for.

My wife underwent surgery three days later. I still have the images very sharp in my memory. (The old carpenter's voice vibrates with emotion. He tries to hide his joy. He swallows with difficulty, while his eyes get teary.) While I was waiting at the corridor next to the operating room, I saw a woman in surgical clothes coming towards me. She told me that Dr. Bălănescu stopped the intervention speechlessly. He closed the doors of his practice and did not want to receive anyone anymore. I looked at her, I did not understand. Why? What was happening? I suspected that she read my mind because she answered my thought with two words. "A miracle!" No tumor was found after the incision. My wife healed inexplicably from a life-threatening cancer. When I visited Father Arsenie shortly thereafter, he was waiting for me with a smile. "Have you now witnessed the power of God? Do you trust me now?" How could I have ever doubted him?

(George interrupts his story. His gaze wanders off to the window through which his wife walks. She takes care of the flowers in the yard of their home. I am a speechless witness to a 'wonderful' miracle, the result of a life-giving confidence and full of hope. Moments later George recalls his story.)

However, that was not all. A friend of mine also became seriously ill. He got admitted in the hospital at Azuga. The skin of his face turned black. The doctors were desperate. They estimated my friend's life expectancy at two months only. I advised my friend to leave the hospital and to visit Father Arsenie with me. He agreed although with reservation and without any hope of healing. We were welcomed by Father Arsenie in the garden. Just like last time, Father Arsenie kept talking about how he spent his days and what his plans for the future were.

At the end of the visit, he said goodbye to me and my friend. He put his hand on his chest and stomach and spoke to him confidently: "Do not worry about your illness. It will not get you small!" That was it. We left home. My friend did not return to the hospital. A few days after our visit to Father Arsenie, he was back on his feet. He is still alive and, despite his age, in perfect health. His healing happened before the revolution in 1989. He knew no health problems since then.

Of course I was at the funeral of Father Arsenie. He was my best friend. How could I not be present? That day I was the last of the long march that came to say goodbye to him at the grave on the hilltop. I still go there often, just like in the old days. I am glad I still can. I feared for a long time that I could no longer do that. I continued to work in the Prislop monastery. For years now, I have seen thousands of pilgrims visit the grave of Father Arsenie, with their questions, fears and desires. Some told me their wonderful story. Monks also testified about their deliverance from temptation or trial. Father Arsenie does not refuse anyone. On the contrary, as he had promised me, he seems to be working with even more force from the Other World. I also still feel his presence the same way as on that day when I worked on the roof. Only now he is no longer watching and talking. He lies on the hill. I go there often, don't say much, put my hands on the wooden cross, and pray silently on my knees.

Recently, I got sick. The doctors at the hospital examined me, but they could not find anything. The pain in my legs was hardly tolerable and did not go away. I told myself I should go to Father Arsenie's grave one last time and say goodbye to my friend, straight to the cross I made for him. I left the hospital with great difficulty and travelled to Prislop. It was an agony. I have grown old. I knelt down by the cross, asked Father Arsenie for forgiveness. I told him that this was the last time I shall visit him and that from then on I would address him from my studio, my garden, or my home. Then there was silence. I could not think anymore. I was done. Everything became clear. I can say goodbye, satisfied. No, it was unquestionably more than this: I was at deep peace with myself. When I got up, I felt how the pain disappeared from my legs and knees. "What is happening? How is this possible?" Without any effort and without any pain I descended from the steep hill to the monastery buildings, which rest in the surrounding silence of the forests and rocks. I looked at the cloudy sky with wondering eyes. Everything was heavenly and perfect although only for a short moment. The fallen world will soon wait. My legs and knees, on the other hand, were healed.

That day is in the distant past, but I remember it as if it was yesterday. Since then, I have lived on without any pain and together with Father Arsenie. We have become inseparable. I talk to him when I work the wood in my small work place, as I chatted with him for days when he came to visit here. I talk to him in the garden when pulling out the weeds or watering the flowers and bushes, or when I am doing nothing. I feel his presence, but in another way. I do know that Father Arsenie is present, that he hears and sees me. A fire illuminates in my heart that will only douse off when we see each other again.

I loved Father Arsenie sincerely and I still do. My desire will and can only be satisfied when I meet him again on the other side, like he promised me. I trust him on his word as I have always trusted him, from the moment we met.

Source: Magazine Formula-As, 2013, no. 1057

**Father
DIONISIE IGNAT
Hieromonk**

Dionisie Ignat was born on 19 July 1963 in Cisnădie (Sibiu) where he is currently a hieromonk at the Elias Monastery in The Albac (Alba).

I was on my first year in Theology in Sibiu when Bishop Serafim, who at the time also was my confessor at the Theological Institute, advised me to spend a few weeks of the summer vacation at the Sâmbăta Monastery. At the time, my friend Maria Silaghi had been suffering from multiple sclerosis for 17 years already. I often offered her a helping hand by pushing her cart or carrying her on my back. The stairs were always a problem for her, so a church building was often not accessible for her. Two days before my departure to Sâmbăta, I visited her and told her about my forthcoming trip. I asked her if she would like to accompany me. 'Of course,' she exclaimed in reply. I knew then that she really wanted to go to the water source.

It was the morning of Friday, 3 August 1990. Maria had confessed and received Holy Communion during the Mass. Then she received the anoiting with blessed oil. In the afternoon, she got ready to go to Father Arsenie's water source, which was located a few miles away. Around 2:30 p.m., however, the weather turned gloomy, a strong wind was blowing, and heavy thunderclouds were forming. Maria thought it was better to postpone the visit to the water source, but I thought that was not a good idea. 'God and Father Arsenie will help us.' The threat of rain should not interfere with our original plans.

We were on our way a little later. We made slight progress given our slow pace. At the place where we had to cross the small river, a car stopped by the side of the road and blocked our passage. A few workers talked about how they could solve their problem. Maria wanted to return because she was ashamed that the workers would see how I would carry her further on my back. I, however, did not want to give up. I had to bring her to the water source. We made a small detour. I pushed Maria in her cart to the height where the source was located. I then took Maria in my arms and carried her a few meters up until we reached the water source. The cart remained unguarded on the road.

Maria washed her face, her hands, and legs. Together we said a few prayers and brought some water with us. When we wanted to leave, an old lady arrived who also washed in the water and filled some plastic bottles. Moments later, a noisy group of visitors reached the holy place. The peaceful pause was broken. Maria and I had nothing to do there anymore. When I wanted to pick her up, she refused yet again. "I do not want these people to see how you carry me on your back. I will hold on to you until we reach my cart."

Maria walked next to me, all the way to the cart. Then she said: "I feel no pain in my legs, I feel power. Let's go to the road where we have to cross the stream and where the car stood still. I have noticed how you pushed me over the boulders and gravel in the cart with great difficulty. Now you can rest a bit, I really feel good." From there, we descended and crossed the stream. Maria kept walking on her own all the way to the monastery where Sister Juliana and Sister Anna, amazed and inspired, welcomed us with open arms. That evening Maria got muscle pain and became bedridden. The next day, she stayed in bed all day. On Sunday, she again attended the Mass, standing up and without any help. Since that day, the cart has remained unused. It was a silent witness of a miracle. God and Father Arsenie truly help the people.

How is Maria? Maria now lives with her sister in the Skete on the Retezat Mountain. Bishop Daniil Stoenescu has housed them there.

An excerpt from the book 'Părintele Arsenie Boca, un om mai presus de oameni' (Father Arsenie Boca, a person above people), Publisher Agaton, Volume 4, 2011.

SEVER VOINESCU
Lawyer and Publicist

Sever Voinescu was born in Ploiesti on 19 June 1969. He graduated from the Law Faculty of the University of Bucharest where he is a member of the Order of Lawyers of Bucharest. Between 1998 and 2000, he was Secretary General of the Ministry of Foreign Affairs. From March 2000 to December 2003, he was the General Consul of Romania in Chicago. From 1 January 2016, he was the editor of the cultural weekly magazine 'Dilema Veche' (The Old Dilemma). That same year, he made the weekly program 'Europa Christiana' (The Christian Europe) for Trinitas-TV. He also published dozens of articles in various magazines and newspapers.

A monk on The Athos Mountain told me that, whoever wants to understand the current state of the Church, must closely follow the phenomenon of modern-day saints. Who are they? What are they learning? How do they live? Why are they acknowledged and recognized as saints by people?

That is why I am so fascinated by Father Arsenie Boca. For more than 25 years, there have been thousands of believers who worship him, ask for his counsel or help and put themselves under his guidance to find the truth. No one, no matter how intelligent, can ignore this signal. Father Arsenie is a man of God. Multitudes of people have experienced this from his early years as a monk. From 1945 onwards, the believers called him 'the Saint from Transylvania.' He was only 35 years old at the time.

He spent his time on earth in almost a perfect way. Anyone who submerges himself or herself in Father Arsenie's life, reads and studies his writings, soon realizes that during his life he has embodied the wonderful paradox of holiness. On the one hand, there is the heavy aspect of suffering, the defamation, and the persecution. On the other hand, there is the wingend grace with which he seems to transcend this burden and through which he remains an example of optimism and hope for other human beings.

Every saint, man or woman, shows how faith in Jesus Christ is a source of power, with which every human situation of powerlessness, misery, or pain can be contained. That is why every life story of a saint is a variation of the same theme, namely love. Anyone who truly believes in God also feels deeply and indestructibly connected to everything and everyone in the created reality. If God Himself sends His Son out of love to take on all the sins of humankind by dying on the cross, if only to free all peoples from the burden of guilt, how can a follower of Christ still hate? Father Arsenie once wrote: "The love of God for the greatest sinner is infinitely greater than the love of the greatest saint for God." This realization is a reason for gratitude and commitment. The deeper the faith is rooted, the more intense the love becomes.

Father Arsenie has undergone and endured numerous insults during his life. He was thrown into prison, forbidden to continue his life as a monk and as a priest, defamed by 'colleagues' from the clergy and was made a suspect by the Security, the security police. Nonetheless, nothing could touch him. Nothing could shake him. He continued to bear witness to his faith, showing The Path without any hesitation. He protected the people with his inner, spiritual power. "*I want to turn your tears from sadness into joy. I will be able to realize more for you after my death than I can now, during my life.*" These are words that illustrate his endless commitment and boundless love for people. His charisma has never faded. His grace has never disappeared. He remained the lovable monk who attracted young people, adults and the elderly, the rich and the poor, the wise and the simple. That Father Arsenie still inspires hundreds of thousands of believers to prayer and good works can only be described as an act of God.

When Pope John Paul II was buried, tens of thousands of people on St. Peter's Square started chanting his name and calling out 'Santo subito.' People begged the authorities within the Roman Catholic Church for an immediate canonization of the deceased Bishop of Rome. This resulted in Pope Benedict XVI asking the designated authorities of the Catholic Church to start the application for canonization, despite the traditional conditions.

For decades, Romanian Orthodox Christians have been similarly asking to declare Father Arsenie as holy. The Church hears their voice, but does not listen (at least for now). Canonization is not a posthumous distinction for the services rendered, but rather a thanksgiving for what someone in the field of faith has meant for humankind. That is why such a massive call is not merely a question, but even more, a confirmation. (...)

However, the destiny of the Christian Faith on earth is only partly linked to or dependent on the Church. The people would rather listen to the voice of Heaven than to the voice of the Church or of the political government. After all, the heart is more receptive than the ear. When the government tried to put Father Arsenie on non-active, thousands of people still continued to visit him. This is proven not only by the testimonies of the visitors, but also from the archives of the Security who was infuriated by the ineffable success of Father Arsenie. Also today it appears that spiritual grace, as well as holiness, is not recognized or granted by a patriarchal decision. Only a signature can officially confirm it.

This is why I repeat:

"Santo Subito! Sfânt imediat! Immediately declare holy!"

An excerpt from the book 'Altfel despre Părintele Arsenie Boca, in convorbiri realizate de Marius Vasileanu' (Another view on Father Arsenie Boca, in conversations made by Marius Vasileanu), pp. 253-258, Editura Şcoala Ardeleană, Cluj Napoca, 2016.

DUMITRU CONSTANTIN-DULCAN
Professor, Psychiatrist-Neurologist

Prof. Dulcan, in addition to being a university professor, psychiatrist and neurologist, is also the author of many books and essays. "The Intelligence of Matter" is a bestseller, awarded in 1992 with the 'Vasile Conta' prize by the Romanian Academy. He holds in high regard the teachings of Father Arsenie Boca, as proven by this quote: "If Father Arsenie's advice could prevent a future illness, then as a doctor I have always done everything to follow his advice, even though the illness or its symptoms were still unknown to me then..."

Doctor Dumitru Constantin-Dulcan, in Romania there are only a few scientists who investigate (almost) inexplicable psychological and spiritual phenomena. How do you see Vader Arsenie Boca from your experience as a scientist and researcher?

From a scientific perspective, I must say that Father Arsenie is a curious case lying on the borderline between the natural and the supernatural and is therefore also an attractive and interesting subject to study. It is of course of great importance here to make a distinction between fact and fiction. That is why it is exceptional to realize that Father Arsenie Boca was a contemporary. He lived and suffered among the peoples of the 20th and 21st centuries, and they can testify today about who he was and what he did. That he often talked about supernatural laws that could transcend the laws of classical science is a difficult challenge. Can we explain the experiences of people who came into contact with Father Arsenie Boca? What is the truth for us, scientists? What do these facts tell us from an objective, scientific point of view?

If even one single testimony is really true, then I will be obliged to accept that there is another reality that I must try to understand and explain even though this reality exceeds the limits of the physical world. It is and remains our duty to investigate facts and to attempt to come to a hypothesis and decision-making after the investigation.

I interviewed people who met him or even knew him well and lived with him together. I am grateful for that. Unfortunately, I did not have the opportunity to meet him myself.

May I conclude from these words that you have investigated whether certain miracles have really happened?

Yes, that is a correct conclusion. I wanted to know where the boundary was, between the initial experience and the final account thereof, what happened and how is it experienced and passed on. That's how I contacted George Vâlcea from Comarnic. I visited him at home, talked to him and his wife. I let them tell their experiences and confronted them with my doubt.

George was a talented woodworker who could also handle unusual tasks. His job often consisted of carrying out special designs. One day, he received an assignment from the monastic sisters in Sinaia. These godly women lived together in a house after they were banned from their monastery. George was shown design drawings that were of exceptional quality, not comparable with the usual sketches. Father Arsenie who led his life in complete anonymity, drew those designs. Moments later, George met Father Arsenie who asked him never to speak to him by name, but always with 'old man'.

This encounter grew over the years into a deeply experienced friendship, making George a unique source to talk about the miracles that happened around and through Father Arsenie. George had a neighbor. He was 26 years old and was very ill. The diagnosis was stomach cancer at a terminal stage. The doctors in the hospital were desperate. They could not think of any further treatment that offered any chance of survival. Because there were wonderful stories circulating about Father

Arsenie, George brought his neighbor to Father Boca who first stared at heaven, as if he were consulting someone.

(This is also confirmed by Nicolae Mărgineanu who directed a film about Father Arsenie Boca.) Afterwards he looked at the cancer patient, drew a line from the chest to the abdomen with his right index finger and said: "That's good. You are healed..." It sounded unbelievable. I therefore also expressed my doubts to George and he immediately invited me to visit his neighbor and let him tell his story.

Another incomprehensible story is that of the funeral of Creştina, the mother of Father Arsenie who was imprisoned during those days in the labor camp at Cernavodă where he and his fellow prisoners were obliged to help dig a channel between the Danube and the Black Sea. He enjoyed the trust of the supervisors who therefore asked him to manage the bookkeeping of the prison. One day, Father Arsenie asked them if he could withdraw into his cell for two hours. He was allowed to. However, when the two hours was over and the supervisors searched Father Arsenie in his cell, no one appeared to be present. Immediately, a loud alarm was sounded. Escape was a serious matter and could never be tolerated. It soon became apparent that the assumption was incorrect: Father Arsenie was lying on the floor with his eyes closed, next to the fence and inside the enclosure. He seemed to be meditating. When the guards woke him up, Father Arsenie looked at them surprised:

 - Oh! Yes, what am I doing...? Can you leave me alone for a

little while longer? She is being buried now.

- Buried? Who is being buried now?

- My mother!

- What? What does that mean?

- I was at my mother's funeral service in Hălmagiu, next to Brad in the Western Mountains.

That was impossible. No one on earth could ever travel back and forth to Brad unnoticed within a two-hour period. However, when contact was made by telephone with the local police in Brad, the story of Father Arsenie was indeed confirmed. He was at his mother's funeral. That means that Father Arsenie had the gift of bilocation: he could be in two places at the same time.

This phenomenon is indeed rare, but it also occur with other saints...

Yes, indeed. What fascinates me is finding out how such phenomena can be explained within the workings of the universe.

George Vâlcea told me another, very remarkable story. Zian Boca prayed on his way to school to God. He was then a 12-year old, very religious boy and asked God what he should do with his life. A few days later, the boy meets an old man on the same road who starts talking to him: "You prayed to God with the question what you should do with your life? This is

150

the answer, as I speak on behalf of God. He lets you know that you must help Him to keep the world in balance. The world is turning, the world is going mad. Life has become relentlessly hard."

That is a particularly interesting fact because from this I can deduce that, according to the Plan from Above, we are actually finding ourselves in a survival mode and we are in spiritual need of people who, through their prayer, keep the world in balance.

Also, Dan Lucinescu tells something remarkable. He, too, had serious reservations about Father Arsenie. How was it possible that a monk could know the name of a visitor he has never met? How can he know about his origins, his illnesses, and even more, his future? It seemed unlikely to him that something like this could happen in this world. That is why, as a scientist, he went on to investigate and made a visit. He went to Sâmbăta de Sus where Father Arsenie worked as a young monk and received hundreds of young adults during the weekends for catechesis and evangelism.

Dan consciously kept a distance to be able to see everything. He saw how the attractive monk, with his penetrating gaze, made an impression on the young people, especially on the girls. An evil thought even occurred –flattery, temptation. At a certain moment, Father Arsenie interrupted his lesson for a short break, and with a detour, approached the unsuspecting Dan.

- "Dan. Tell me... Do you really think I am a cheater?"

I must mention that before this happened, Dan had prayed to God to help him understand this phenomenon.

I also want to mention a few things that I saw in a movie about Father Arsenie, for example, about a 16-year old girl in a wheelbarrow.

You are now referring to the film "Father Arsenie Boca, A Man of God", directed by Nicolae Mărgineanu?

Indeed, yes. It is about the story of a 16-year old girl who was brought by her father, a farmer, to the monastery of Father Arsenie in a wheelbarrow. She was unable to walk due to child paralysis that occurred after brain inflammation, as a result of which the brain nerves could no longer pass on signal stimuli to start learning to walk and move. Father Arsenie asked the farmer to let his daughter stay at the monastery for a few days.

Witnesses later confirmed that after a few days, they saw the girl walking next to Father Arsenie. That is impossible from a medical point of view. Nobody can explain that in a logical way. That makes such a case particularly fascinating for me because as a neurologist, I am responsible for people who suffer from such an affliction.

Such an incident proves beyond doubt that a certain dimension exists, apparently a spiritual dimension, that transcends our reality. The question that arises in me is: How is it possible that a man, Father Arsenie Boca in this case, is able to heal other people when that is not possible for modern medicine?

A second question to which I would like to find an answer was, how can someone know the name of someone he or she has never met? Where can you find, read or search for it on earth or in the universe? On the forehead?

Could it be that Father Arsenie came into contact with someone who had the gift of hypnosis during his youth or during his education? I do not believe that, but in certain circles such slander is liked and often spread. I assume that you also have the necessary knowledge and experience to take an objective and wise opinion.

We have to be careful on this point and separate the reality from an apparent reality that is the case with hypnosis or placebo medicine. However, a healing miracle with Father Arsenie happens, and that is easy to observe and derive, on a purely physiological level. Knowing your name, your past, your illnesses and your future has nothing to do with hypnosis or delusions or suggestion. It is reality. He actually healed or gave advice to avert an impending disease.

Subsequently, what happened (and still happens) with Father Arsenie is not exceptional, but occasionally occurs in the Church. In the second part of my book "The Search for a Lost Meaning" (Eikon, Cluj-Napoca, 2008), I tell, as a neurologist, about the life story of Stavros Kalkandis, a pilot from World War II, in which he was badly wounded. His spine was damaged, resulting in interrupted contact between the brain and certain muscles. Because of this, he could no longer move his hands and feet. He stayed in this paralyzed condition for 24 years in a shelter for the wounded or disabled soldiers. Several times he went on a pilgrimage to Egina (Greece) where Saint Nectarius is buried. During such a pilgrimage, he prayed to the saint: "I did not come here to ask anything, but to give something. I offer you my life. Do what you think makes sense with it." During his return, he feels how his body is 'defrosting' and he feels a sort of life energy flowing through his motionless hands and feet. He asks the doctors on duty the next day at 8 a.m. to be present at his bedside. At that moment, with all the doctors as witnesses, he effortlessly got up from his bed after 24 years and started walking.

I know that hypnosis, suggestion, or placebo cannot achieve this. I know how ingenious and robust a cervical vertebra is built, how the nerves through the vertebrae, which function as 2-cm thick tunnels, transmit signals from the brain to the muscles. I can only confirm that such a cure is not the result of a conscious medical intervention. It is worth mentioning that this soldier was even treated by President Roosevelt's personal doctor! He kept him in his sanatorium for years to be able to follow his healing process closely. When he took him out from the sanatorium, he entrusted him with the following:

- Friend, I have invited the best doctors around your sick bed. No one was able to give you any improvement. Only one doctor is left.
- Who?
- God.

That is what happened after 24 years. God completely healed this man through a miraculous intervention by Saint Nectarius of Egina. There is no room for rational explanations or interpretations here. There is only room for a humble acknowledgment that a certain kind of force was at work here that transcends our knowledge.

Can you make certain connections or distinguish similarities between the events around Father Arsenie and Saint Nectarius of Egina?

Absolutely! I would like to admit here that for my scientific research, I have travelled several times not only to Egina in Greece, but also to France (Lourdes) and to Brazil (Aparecida)[1]. I wanted to know for sure whether what was told corresponded to what had actually happened. In addition to testimonials, I also consulted scientific literature. In Lourdes, for example, scientific reports are prepared after the verification of a miracle. Also, American doctors are involved in this process to prevent any bias. Moreover, it must be said that the Roman Catholic Church is more sceptical than the Orthodox in recognizing a miracle.

Why was Petrache Lupu investigated during the interwar period by Doctor George Marinescu, but is there no work being done by a permanent scientific committee of doctors and psychologists to investigate the miracles that take place, for example, at the grave of Father Arsenie?

That is a more than justified question. Petrache Lupu was the 17-year old shepherd boy who received a vision from an old man at a willow tree in Maglavit, was asked by the old man to advise people to turn to God and also performed miracles

at the time. He was indeed investigated by George Marinescu,

---

1 Lourdes is the main sanctuary of Mary in France. All the many miracles that are attested there are examined by a scientific committee that has conducted exemplary rigorous work of examination. Aparecida (Nossa Senhora Aparecida) is a Brazilian sanctuary of Mary that has existed since 1717. That year, empty-handed fishermen cast their nets for the last time and took out a small terracotta statue of the Mother of God. It was venerated in the oratory of one of the fishermen, after which a chapel was built for it in 1734, and, ahead of the influx of the faithful and the great number of miracles, a new church was built in 1834.

a renowned neurologist, and was declared completely healthy and normal. Today, the world has changed. There is scepticism and secularization. Many domains in which the Church used to be active have now been taken over by science. A lot has changed since around 1850 when Darwin's theory of evolution put the Church's creation theory under pressure. All too often, scientific thinking has been placed in opposition to religious thinking and that is still the case today, with technological evolution and secularization still and increasingly the case.

This is probably also the reason that there is still no medical commission. Moreover, Father Arsenie is not the only monk or priest who did miracles. Saint Augustine described a miracle as something of which we know nothing yet. Does that not mean that sooner or later we can and will discover the true nature of a miracle?

That is exactly the purpose of my research, which was not limited to the Christian Churches. I was visiting an Indian hospital where I met a six-year old child who was dumb and deaf. He was following a traditional, therapeutic treatment. One day, he stood behind a doctor's desk and unexpectedly asked: "What are you doing there?" Incredibly beautiful, impressive! From which we must conclude that such phenomena are not limited solely to the Orthodox Faith, not even to the Christian Faith.

I think I can conclude from this that there is an extra dimension, in which certain laws apply and certain forces are active. If a person respects these laws, then he can also use the powers, causing miracles to happen. That seems to me to be a correct, scientific decision. I was not interested in the mysticism of any religion, but the wonderful phenomena that manifested and manifest. That is scientific research.

I hereby take the opportunity to frame this in the history of scientific research itself. Initially, there was the investigation of nature itself. This research was based on Newton's findings, which laid the foundations for classical physics based on the perception of forces.

Gradually, the study shifted or deepened into the domain of atoms and molecules. Later, this domain evolved into something beyond the atomic and molecular structure and is no longer perceptible as such, namely quantum physics, in which matter no longer has the properties of a solid form, but of a field. That is exactly the distinction between the physical world and the transcending, spiritual dimension, the 'Source of All Life.' (...)

Father Arsenie showed a great interest in the control of human (physical and mental) motivations by the person's will. Herewith, he also compared the mystique of different religions. He wanted to show that the willpower and conscience were really able to consciously control the instincts, reflexes or passions.

That is correct, but perhaps the terminology is somewhat less adequate for our time. We distinguish two levels in human behavior, namely the rational-cognitive and the emotional-affective level. Father Arsenie searched for the optimal relationship between the rational and emotional level, between a reasoned and an instinctive lifestyle. Generally speaking, the rational approach to life is of a higher order than the emotional approach, just as a person essentially surpasses the animal.

What can we conclude when we look from this perspective at the 'achievements' of Father Arsenie, Padre Pio, Nectarius of Egina and many others? Perhaps it is too personal a point of view. Maybe, my explanation is too subjective, but for me it is very believable because it is based on scientific studies on quantum physics, neurology and transpersonal psychology, which have been on the rise since 1975 (and later again in 1992).

I believe, from a scientific viewpoint, that there is a fundamental, ethical law on which the universe is based, through which our human brain also functions. It is impossible to attribute other assets to the universe than to the human brain. Water and ice are the same substance but in different forms. In my book 'Codul Etic de Funcţionalitate a Creierului Uman' (The Ethical Code of Functionality of the Human Brain), published in 2008, I come to the conclusion that the universe is understood and propagated by the human brain and that the underlying law is ethical in nature, which must and can be respected by every person, regardless of the religion he or she adheres to. This ethics vibrates in harmony with the universe and therefore also contains a universal force. Anyone who is able to develop this power within himself or herself by following the ethical law (not hating, doing good and the like), rises above the everyday human level and transforms himself or herself into what we call today 'a saint'. (...)

It is clear and self-evident that human thoughts also determine the physical condition. Those who cherish good, positive thoughts, live in peace with themselves, their fellow human beings, the world and the universe and stimulate the inner, physical forces, and also the connecting forces with fellow human beings and society. Thoughts of envy, hatred, revenge and violence, on the other hand, are destructive to everyone and everything. Then we come back to an earlier statement: the term 'field' within the positive sciences and their characteristics. Something similar occurs in the field of our human thoughts. Werner Heisenberg says about this: "Even the smallest thought penetrates the furthest corner of the Universe." That means that every wave of thought, positive or negative, has an effect on everything and everyone: on myself, my fellow humans beings, society, the world, the universe. (...)

However, the interpretation of this law is also reversible. What others think or say also has consequences for us. Then, it suddenly becomes very clear what the impact is of the contemporary media and of the political circus, nationally and internationally. Humans are constantly attacked by (mainly negative) stimuli, which affect their DNA, their nervous system and their immune system, which immediately has consequences for the quality and duration of their life.

What do saints do? They avoid the harmful and worldly ballast, they live in harmony with themselves, fellow human beings, the world and the universe. Is it then surprising that they can realize what science cannot achieve? Do I still have to wonder about the achievements of Father Arsenie Boca, Padre Pio, Nectarius of Egina or Serafim of Sarov?

Father Arsenie has nothing to do with hypnosis. He learned 'the secret' of a sacred life on the Mountain of Athos. I also visited this mountain and I met monks who spent their remaining time praying after their hard day's work, often until late in the night with a minimum of food and drink. During the time of Father Arsenie, life on the Athos was undoubtedly even harder! We should be concerned about them and about their miserable living situations. However, they pray for us, for the society, for the world and the universe.

Certainly, it is not the science that saves the world from destruction or ruin, but their vital prayer! We must be grateful to them and take them as an example. However, I must immediately admit: I do not go to church daily or weekly. I don't even argue for the Church. Rather, I argue for scientific knowledge. I also do not want to argue against the Church. As a scientist, I only want to understand why some people are healed in a wonderful, not medically controlled way.

I want to tell you this concrete story that George Vâlcea from Comarnic entrusted to me. One day, Father Arsenie came to visit and brought some pastries. He told George that he was leaving on a journey. He pointed upwards. He assured him that he would not leave George, but would, on the contrary, help him more often and more intensely. He advised George to visit his grave in Prislop later. He did that, too. With the last visit, he was healed from his unbearable knee pain...

Do you understand? Father Arsenie told the same as Seraphim van Sarov: "Come to my grave! Then and there I can help you more than I could ever do during my life...!" These are similarities that nobody cannot ignore. It is clear that both had understood the spiritual depths or had reached the spiritual heights. There is no doubt about that. Is it not logical that both saints could talk to the animals (birds, bear), just as Francis of Assisi also did? I have also been to Assisi. I have visited many places where strange phenomena or saints have manifested themselves. I was and am not interested in newspaper articles, but in scientific reports. I am fascinated by the truth, not the sensation.

Father Arsenie Boca has followed a few courses with the professor of medicine and anatomy Francisc Rainer. In the book 'The Path to the Kingdom' some chapters with such texts from Father Arsenie were included. What do you think about such statements, pieces of advice, or remarks?

Let us be very clear about this. Father Arsenie knew much more than what we do at this point. We only know the strictly material and perceptible. Father Arsenie had a fuller picture of the fact, a total picture of what man is, what life has as its purpose. That truth is spiritual in nature. What we have discovered and are still discovering is insufficient. What Father Arsenie offers us is a surplus, an added value. We cannot reject or question this complementary offer. If he gave advice on how to prevent a certain disease, why should I as a doctor reject this advice? Is prevention not much better than cure? Of course! As a doctor, once the disease has manifested itself, we must all too often limit ourselves to fighting the symptoms or reducing the disease, without, however, having any assurance to completely remove the disease.

I strongly believe that Father Arsenie Boca saw a kind of personal field among people. Others might call it an 'aura'. Father Arsenie was able to read this field and also give beneficial advice from this knowledge. Maybe, he saw upcoming germs as spots, or maybe not. However, I really think that by complying with the underlying ethical law, he could use the creative power of the universe in a wonderful way.

Our world is too materialistic and too ambitious. Our thoughts are too limited, our ideals too personal – name, fame, power, money, comfort. We are not in harmony with the created universe and with the Creator.

Isn't it amazing to see Father Arsenie performing the miracles that Jesus Christ showed twenty centuries ago? What's more, we are contemporaries with this man! Certain stories about Jesus are dismissed as purely symbolic, or even worse, pure fantasy. Here and now we have testimonies from people who have been through such experiences themselves. Is that not the necessary lifebuoy to keep doubting generations on board – with a scientifically correct research and report?

Is there therefore no need for an interdisciplinary committee composed of doctors, psychologists, anthropologists, theologians and scientists who study such phenomena from their own professionalism and report on their personal findings together?

Of course! It is from this necessity and inspiration that I started my investigation, not out of naivety. I have searched for answers from these real phenomena that have led me to a spiritual reality in which our daily-life physics is embedded. We cannot deny this reality. I truly believe that this reality has points of similarity with quantum physics, but also with experiences of near-death and the hereafter. It has to do with experiencing another dimension of the same reality, with field, waves and particles.

At the same time, this observation is also comprehensive and all-determining. It is about vague concepts like good and evil, life and death, matter and spirit, survival and destruction, time and eternity, sinner and saint, perpetrator and victim, but also about politics, communication media, technology and morality.

Is it a mission of the Church to make such phenomena discussable and to make them available and translate this into a contemporary language?

Doubtless. There, Church and science can meet again. There, we have a common goal, far beyond mere curiosity.

This is perhaps a delicate question, but did you also have a personal experience with Father Arsenie during your investigation?

No, I did not. However, I do have experiences that exceed the limits of time and space. I don't really know if I can put these into words. An example might create some clarity. I am with you, as now, in a conversation. Suddenly, I realize, in one second, what will happen to me tomorrow. No suspicion, no expectation, but a certain knowledge. No fact, but a lived feeling, as if a pre-deflection of time could be felt. There were also symbolic dreams when I fought against a deadline in 1989. For example, I found myself with two colleagues in an extremely uncomfortable situation on a desolate, in a snowy field in Germany. The peculiar thing was that I immediately knew how to translate these symbolic dream situations into concrete, real problems as though a veil were being lifted between the worlds of dreams and reality...

I also have the feeling that without such experiences I could never have conducted my research or could never have experienced this interview. It almost seems as if I were a part of a spiritual plan, as though someone were taking me by the hand and guiding me to those places where I can find an answer or where I had to do something. When that happens, it is confirmed by – yes, the universe or by an inner voice. In any case, there is an undeniable and unquestionable certainty that everything is good. Nobody can take that away from me or deny me that, not even by death threats. Such an experience means much more than having, reading, or understanding a library of books. Such an experience is stronger than the most beautiful theory. This experience has taught me that the truth commands me to testify about a deeper and higher reality than the reality in which we find ourselves in our daily life.

I have heard that you have met many clergymen, including Orthodox Christian hierarchs who were very fond of your research and your writings.

Absolutely. I have a very friendly relationship with many priests. I am not categorically opposed to Orthodoxy, which my mother confesses. The answer to the frequently asked question, as a scientist, how I feel about the Orthodox Church or the Orthodox Faith, is actually very simple: science is cognitive-rational, religion is mainly affective-emotional. My research showed and taught me that science and belief are not necessarily contradictory, as has been claimed for centuries, but rather they complement each other. Nobody can ever deny that God exists!

An excerpt from the book 'Altfel despre Părintele Arsenie Boca, in convorbiri realizate de Marius Vasileanu' (Another view on Father Arsenie Boca, in conversations made by Marius Vasileanu), pp. 227-252, Editura Școala Ardeleană, Cluj-Napoca, 2016.

GERMINA GEORGETA PUNGA-HERBRETEAU
Teacher and Broker

Germina was born in Romania where she worked as a teacher. She has been living in the Netherlands for more than 25 years now. She works as a real estate agent and paints icons during her spare time.

A convinced Orthodox Christian, she is particularly fascinated by insights into the spiritual life. As a tireless pilgrim on the path called 'life', she was responsible for the publication of 'The Path to the Kingdom', in Dutch, a compilation of texts by Father Arsenie Boca, which had previously been published in Romanian and English.

I first met Father Arsenie during the summer of 2010. At the time, I was completely overwhelmed by reading a book which I received as a gift from a friend. I immediately decided to travel to Romania in September and visited Father Arsenie's grave. On September 25, I was supposed to attend a child's baptism and a relative suggested that I should travel on October 2. to the monastery in Prislop where Father Arsenie is buried. However, the return flight to the Netherlands was already booked on October 4. There was really little time to visit the

Prislop monastery.

I felt very worried, inside I knew it had to be different. A few days later, I was still reading a bit about Father Arsenie at my desk on my computer screen. It was well after midnight when I discovered that he was born on 29 September 1910. That meant that his centenary would soon be celebrated and I wanted to be present there. My sleep was very restless that night. I could barely wait until the morning to call my godson to ask him if he could take me to Prislop with his car. He works as a taxi driver. That was no problem at all: "Of course, godmother! I will take you wherever you wish to be!"

So it happened that a few days after the baptism, I went to Prislop where I spent the night on September 28, allowing me to attend the Divine Liturgy that would be celebrated on September 29 at 8.00 a.m. at the monastery church. It was an indescribable miracle. I was able to celebrate the centenary with thousands of people where Father Arsenie himself lived and painted the icons of Christ and the Mother of God who could (and still can) be worshipped there.

After the Liturgy, two priests testified about their experiences and encounters with Father Arsenie. Also, I felt the urge to tell people how wonderful it was that I was at this celebration of the centenary. I prayed to God for a sign that I, too, might testify although I did not dare to speak in public. Then, Father Petru Vamvulescu said: "If someone among you feels called to tell something, don't be afraid." I considered this as an answer to my prayer, so I went forward and described how touched I was that I was able to experience all this.

After my testimony, I went up the hill where Father Arsenie is buried. The grave is located at the end of the cemetery of the nuns. I knelt by the cross and embraced it with both hands. Then, I saw that I was not wearing my rings. "*Where are my rings?*" As soon as this thought dawned upon me, there was an inner voice that calmed my moment of stress: "*Why are you worried about your rings? Cherish this moment with love and attention because you are here at the grave of Father Arsenie. You really wanted to feel his intimate and inner presence?*" I became calm and a conscious and personal prayer rose from my heart. Heavenwards.

Then, I travelled on to the little church of Drăgănescu where the icons of Father Arsenie overwhelmed me. One icon in particular, that of the Mother of God, moved me in an exceptional way. When I looked at her gaze, an almost indescribable feeling touched me as though Heaven and Earth touched each other and as if Eternity manifested itself in a few seconds. Is this the coming together of what theologians call the 'transcendent' (transcendent, vertical) and the 'immanent' (present, horizontal) aspects of Faith? I felt that Father Arsenie was present at that time and place, and that I was allowed to share in the mutual love between the Mother of God and Father

Arsenie, of which this icon was and is a wordless expression. Then, the tears came like clear spring water, liberating and fresh. It was a moment that I still cherish.

I only remember one other moment that was just as intense. I was in the Pecherska Monastery in Kiev (Ukraine) where I worshipped the little icon of the Mother of God, surrounded by Saints Antonius and Theodosius[1]. The face of the Mother of God can hardly be distinguished, yet I was unexpectedly touched. I let my tears run wild, while intense and abundant joy delighted my soul. I knew that the Mother of God was very close. The guide of the small group I had joined turned to me, leaned towards me and said softly: "You are a happy woman." I can only confirm that – truly.

After this first pilgrimage, I have never let go of Father Arsenie. Neither did he, I suspect, because he had a surprise for me at almost every pilgrimage. When I was in Jerusalem during the first week of January 2011 to celebrate the feast of Basil the Great and the Baptism of Christ, I stayed with my sister at a Romanian nun's place on walking distance of the Holy Sepulchre where I met Father Petru Vamvulescu, whom I had spoken for the first time in Prislop, at Father Arsenie's centenary. Also, he recognized me and gave me the white wool cardigan of Father Arsenie, which I was allowed to wear for a few days such as during our trip to Samaria where we visited

1 Monastery founded in 1051 by two monks from Mount Athos: Saint Anthony the Athonite and Saint Theodosius of Kiev.

the source of Jacob and where Jesus met Fotina. I also wore Father Arsenie's white cardigan during the Liturgy and Water Consecration on the edge of the Jordan where we stood together with Father Petru next to Patriarch Theophiel of Jerusalem and the latter threw the Cross into the water. It was unimaginable to see how the water started to swirl and to flow upstream and how the Spirit was tangibly descending on the crowd.

I had the same experience in the same year during the Holy Week, which precedes Easter. I knew that Father Petru would be there too but we had not made any concrete agreements. I left everything to Father Arsenie in complete confidence. On Tuesday, I went to the Liturgy and Water Consecration near the Jordan River, where once again Patriarch Theophiel of Jerusalem throws the Cross (three times!) into the water, whereupon the miracle repeats itself over and over again. I searched among the countless believers for the silhouette of Father Petru, but I could not see it anywhere. To make matters worse, it appeared that, after the ceremony, I missed my bus. I was left behind with my sisters at the parking lot. Desperate and panicked, I prayed: "Lord, why are you abandoning us here? Father Arsenie, help us!" After only a few minutes of impatiently waiting, a familiar figure approached us. It looked like a mirage, a mirage in the oppressive pressure of a frightening desert. Father Petru! Due to engine trouble, his bus had been seriously delayed. Coincidence or Providence? We could only be grateful and make use of his offer to take us back to our place of residence.

So it happened again and again, even at the mass gatherings in Jerusalem, when the Holy Fire comes down during the Easter Vigil in the church of the Holy Sepulchre, or at the memorial services in Prislop, on the death anniversary of Father Arsenie! How is it possible that Father Petru and I always meet among the thousands of visitors at the same place, without making clear agreements in advance?

After my return from Jerusalem, my life changed. After a devastating divorce, I had lived alone for a number of years, but gradually a relationship deepened with a friendly man. However, I was uncertain. I doubted whether I could or should take the step to marry again, especially when the first disagreements arose. I had no idea what to do. Did I have to end my relationship or continue?

I thought of visiting Father Justin Pârvu at the monastery in Petru Vodă (Romania) to ask him for advice. In my head, I said, and I quote: "Father Arsenie is dead. There is no way to speak to him. I am going to visit Father Justin Pârvu[2]. He is alive." I started planning for the trip to the Petru Vodă Monastery, to go to Romania from the Netherlands, but something prevented me. I could not leave.

---

2 Archimandrite Iustin or Justin Pârvu (1919-2013), renowned spiritual father of the monastery of Petru Vodă.

One night, however, I had an extraordinary dream. I was present in a square where a priest on an elevation spoke and blessed those present. On his head he wore a royal crown, the same as the one placed on the head of the bride and groom during an Orthodox wedding. I called upon the priest and told him that I also wanted to be blessed. He asked me where I was from. I answered him that I was from the Netherlands. He asked me to wait a while because he first had to handle a few other things and then he disappeared into the crowd.

I decided not to leave and to wait for the priest. He returned and approached me. His face was fine and elongated, his eyes penetrating and incredibly beautiful and warm. A blue-orange light danced around him. He looked at me, took my hands and asked me: "*Where are your rings?*" I answered him that I never wore rings on a pilgrimage. He looked at me with a smile and softly tapped my ring finger where I once wore my wedding ring. "I am divorced, Father." "*I know, but why don't you think once also what is good for you? Come with me, I will pray for you!*" We entered a church where the priest knelt and prayed. I felt unworthy and ashamed. I didn't know what to do. Just as I wanted to kneel down, he stood up. He took a serving tray with bread on it. He handed it to me and said: "*Eat, it's blessed!*" Then, I woke up.

Suddenly, I realized: it was Father Arsenie! Only he knows my question, which I asked at the cross on his grave: "*Where are my rings?*"

I am deeply ashamed that I have not asked him for help in prayer.

On 29 September 2012, on Father Arsenie's birthday, my husband and I were married in church.

Those who actually believe and trust in God experience how God's Providence intervenes in the reality of everyday life. He 'accidentally' brings those people or those events on our path of life that can or will be meaningful to us. He is concerned with us down to the smallest things, as is also evident from numerous details of many saints' lives. A bus has engine trouble, a plane leaves half an hour earlier than expected, an appointment is cancelled, which means that a new situation can arise, and so on and so forth. Jesus Himself asks us not to worry: "Aren't two sparrows offered for sale for a penny? Not one of them will fall to the ground without your Father. The hairs of your head are also all counted. Then do not be afraid: you are beyond many sparrows." (Matthew 10,29 - 31)

That is also why I can wholeheartedly endorse and validate what Christians have been witnessing for centuries, namely that a saint is indeed the very best friend for people.

Georgeta Germina Herbreteau-Punga

SHORT BIOGRAPHY

1910 September 29:
Zian Vălean Boca was born in Vața de Sus (Hunedoara), in what was then Austria-Hungary (often referred to as the Austro-Hungarian Empire).

Father: Jozef Petrus Boca (born in Brad on 24 February 1881), shoemaker.
Mother: Creștina Popa (born in Vața de Sus on 30 October 1892), housekeeper.

They were married on 7 November 1909 in Vața de Jos. Joseph was Greek Catholic, Creștina was Orthodox. They moved in with the parents of Creștina, Gligor Popa and Păscuța Mariș on the Bujoara hill in Vața de Sus, which was part of the Hunedoara district in the Transylvania region.

Transylvania was initially, since 1867, part of the Austria-Hungary double monarchy, which was dissolved on 31 October 1918 after a military defeat on the Italian front of the First World War. After the First World War officially ended on 11 November 1918, the Romanian army occupied territories that politically belonged to Hungary, but were populated demographically by a Romanian majority. In August 1919, the Romanian troops invaded the

Hungarian capital Budapest. In June 1920, the
Trianon Treaty declared that the areas with a
Romanian population majority were definitively
allocated to Romania. In Transylvania, the population
was 57.3% Romanian.

1913   March 22:
A second child, a girl, was born in the Boca family.
The sister of Zian was named 'Viorela Minca' and
was baptized on April 6, but died on October 12.

1922   March 22:
Jozef and Creştina got separated for an unknown
reason to us. The divorce decree granted custody
over Zian to the father.

September:
Zian started secondary school at Avram Iancu
College in Brad, where also his cousin Vasile Crucin
(1902-1951), the son of his aunt Anna Boca, sister of
father Joseph, took lessons.

1926   June 19:
Joseph Petrus Boca, the father of Zian, died in Brad.
Zian spent the weekends and holidays at Vasile
Crucin, where he could study the national literature.

1929   June:
Zian finished his secondary studies at Avram Iancu
College in Brad as the primus of all final-year
students. That was why he could plant an oak tree
on the school grounds.

September:
Zian started his education at the Theological Faculty
in Sibiu.

1933 June:
Zian graduated from the Theological Faculty in Sibiu.

September:
Based on the express request and with the
financial support of Metropolitan Nicolae Bălan,
Zian enrolled at the Academy of Fine Arts,
specialization 'Decorative Art', in Bucharest.
Professor Costin Petrescu asked Zian Boca for his
cooperation in painting the entry of Michaël
The Brave in Alba Julia.

Michael the Brave was the prince of Wallachia,
Transylvania and Moldavia. He was the first to succeed
in uniting the three principalities in 1600. This scene
was part of the huge fresco that depicted Romania's
history and measures in total 75m long and 3m high.
It was the largest painting in Romania in those days

and still decorates the auditorium of the Romanian Athenaeum in Bucharest, the concert hall that housed the philharmonic orchestra.

1934 September:
In addition to his classes at the Academy of Fine Arts in Bucharest, Zian Boca was also following the course 'Mysticism and Theology' with Professor Nichifor Crainic at the Theological Faculty in Bucharest and the course 'Anatomy' with Professor Francisc Rainer at the Faculty of Medicine at Bucharest.

1936 September 11:
Zian Boca was ordained deacon in the Sibiu Cathedral.

1938 June:
Zian Boca finished his studies with distinction at the Academy of Fine Arts in Bucharest. He also successfully completed his courses at the Medical and Theological Faculty in Bucharest.

1939   March 12 - June 8:
With the blessing of Metropolitan Nicolae Bălan, Zian
Boca left for Mount Athos, where he immersed
himself in the Orthodox life of the monks. He stayed
there in the Hypatius cell of the Vatopedu Monastery
and worked under the guidance of Father Dometius,
among others, on the construction of a staircase to
the skete Prodomos. While working, he witnessed
a miracle. Moreover, in a vision, the Mother of God
led him to a mountaintop where he met the holy
Seraphim of Sarov, who gave him the gift of
clairvoyance and prophecy.

182

Passport photo (Mount Athos)

June:
Zian Boca moved into the Brâncoveanu Monastery in
Sâmbăta de Sus.

September October:
Zian Boca was doing an internship in Chişinău to
learn the art of gilding and working with gold leaf.

1940 May 3:

Zian Boca was ordained a hierodeacon and monk in the Brâncoveanu Monastery. From this moment, he chose to go through life under the name 'Arsenie', after the Desert father Arsenius the Great (350-450). He immediately started renovating the buildings and redesigning the surrounding gardens.

June:

Serafim Popescu came to join Father Arsenie in the Brâncoveanu Monastery. He was ordained a priest on 20 February 1941 and thereafter on 25 April 1941 a hieromonk.

1942 April 10:

Father Arsenie was ordained as a hieromonk, abbot and priest. He helped Dumitru Stăniloaie, professor of theology, in translating the first volumes of the

Filocalia, a collection of texts from the earliest Church Fathers and monks of the Hesychastic tradition.

Cover design for the Filocalia

1948 May 17:
Father Arsenie was forced to leave the monastery at Sâmbăta de Sus. He was arrested and tortured by the Security, who interrogated him in Făgăraş, from 7 June to 16 June, about possible contacts with opponents of the Communist Regime that he would have met and given shelter in the monastery. After that, he was transferred to the prison of Braşov, known for torturing.

November 25:
Metropolitan Nicolae Bălan personally brought Father Arsenie to the monastery in Prislop (Haţeg, Hunedoara) where he took up residence as an abbot.

1950 April 12:
With the blessing of Bishop Andreas, the monastery
in Prislop became a monastery for a maximum of ten
women, who were spiritually formed and
accompanied by two priests, namely Father Arsenie
Boca and Father Dometie Manolache.

1951 January 16:
Father Arsenie was arrested for the second time,
under provision 150/50 of Sibiu RSP.

January 19:
Father Arsenie was transported to the camp at
Cernavodă, where the prisoners had to dig the canal
between the Danube and the Black Sea.

The Danube-Black Sea Canal runs from Cernavodă
(Danube) to Constanța (southern branch) and
Năvodari (northern branch) and Constanța (southern
branch), the largest and most important port in

Romania. *The canal, which is part of the European canal system that connects the North Sea with the Black Sea, was opened in 1984 and has a length of 64 km. In the past, the sailing distance between Cernavodă and Constanţa was 400 km! The width is 60 m, the depth 7 m. The northern branch has a length of 26.6 km; its width is 50 m and the depth is 5.5 m.*

December 6:
Father Arsenie's mother Creştina died at the age of 59 from cancer in Hălmagiu (Gurahont-Arad). Although Father Arsenie lived in the labor camp at the Black Sea, he still miraculously attended his mother's funeral.

1952   March 17:
Father Arsenie was released from the labour camp at Cernavodă and returned to his monastery in Prislop.

Monastery stamp, designed by Father Arsenie

1955 January 12 - June 12:
Father Arsenie followed an internship in the Galați
Cathedral to be recognized as a decorator of church
buildings by the Romanian Patriarchate.

September 20:
Father Arsenie was arrested for the third time. He was
subsequently interrogated and locked up in the
prisons of Timișoara, Jilava and Oradea.

Arrestatiefoto's en vingerafdrukken

1956 April 7:
Father Arsenie was released from prison in
Oradea.

April 8:
Father Arsenie moved into the Prislop
Monastery again.

1959 May 14:
The monastery in Prislop closed.
Father Arsenie was forbidden by Bishop Andreas
Magieru, Bishop of Arad and Hunedoara to perform
any further spiritual acts. He was also obliged to wear
civilian clothing.

August 7:
Father Arsenie painted with Vasile Rudeanu the
church of Saint Eleutherius in Bucharest.

Mother of God with Christ in prison clothing

1961 February 13:
The work in the Eleutherius Church was being
terminated.

February 14:
The Romanian Patriarchate hired Father Arsenie as
an icon painter in the workshop of the 'Schitul
Maicilor' in Bucharest.
He attended the Divine Liturgy as a choir singer.

1962 Father Arsenie spent his days in Drăgănescu and
Bucharest. However, he was closely monitored by the
Securitate. This photo is proof of this.

1967 June 1:

Father Arsenie ended his work at the Romanian Patriarchate and accepted a new assignment, namely the painting of the interior of the Nicholas church in Drăgănescu (Giurgiu). He had been working on the frescoes for fifteen years and received hundreds of visitors in between.

1976 February 3:

An intelligence report from secret agent 'Tania' showed that "Father Arsenie / Zian Boca was retired and still resided in the Dr. Petrinistraat at house number 2. He was a respected and calm man who led a normal life. He continued to work as a church decorator and can always be found near his home and the church. He wore a beard."

1978 March 11:
Five former monastic sisters asked Father Arsenie to help them build a common home (metoc) in the Nightingale street (Strada Privighetorilor) No. 16 in Sinaia. He was asked to draw designs, which would later be executed in wood by George Vâlcea from Comarnic. Also here, Father Arsenie had a small studio where he occasionally resided and supervised the work.

1983 October 2:
The Nicholas Church in Drăgănescu was blessed and consecrated by the Episcopal Vicar of Patriarch Justin Moisescu of Romania.

1989 November 28:
Father Arsenie died in the monastic establishment in Sinaia.

December 4:
Father Arsenie was buried in the monastery in Prislop.